A YEAR OF

Self-

LOVE

DAILY WISDOM AND INSPIRATION
FOR LOVING YOURSELF

Troy L. Love, LCSW

ROCKRIDGE
PRESS

Interior and Cover Designer: Amanda Kirk
Art Producer: Hillary Frileck
Editor: Eliza Kirby
Production Editor: Erum Khan
Production Manager: Holly Haydash
Author photo courtesy of © Bill Butler

ISBN: Print 978-1-64152-764-4 | eBook 978-1-64152-973-0

This book is dedicated to my children.
Your brilliant light, your talents and energy,
and your love bless my life every day
and inspire me to be better today than
I was the day before.

Contents

Introduction

When I was 19 years old, I came across a saying: "If you don't love yourself, you can't love others." I instantly disagreed with it. In my mind, I was a very loving person. I loved my friends. I loved my family. I loved my teachers. I tried to be nice to everyone who I met. I had a huge smile on my face for all the world to see.

But underneath the surface, I was depressed, suicidal, and filled with shame. I didn't believe that I was lovable at all. Cognitively, I knew that people loved me, but in my heart, I felt that I was unworthy of their love.

Still, I wanted to believe the quote wasn't true, that I could love others anyway. I remember the moment the saying finally made sense to me. I had recently moved away from home and was living with two roommates I barely knew. I felt so lonely and homesick, and I knew something needed to change. I was standing in the bathroom, hiding from the world before I had to go back out and face it. I looked at myself in the mirror. I remember arguing with myself out loud about how this saying could not be true. And then I closed my eyes and became quiet. Something shifted.

A realization began to filter through: *I can love others, even if I don't love myself. But the problem is, if they try to love me back, I will dismiss it, reject it, or push it away until they get tired of trying to convince me that I am worthy of their love, and then I will have the evidence that I am unlovable.*

As I meditated upon that new thought (even though I had no idea what meditation was at the time), I realized that love is an energy meant to be shared. My refusal to take off the mask, show others my pain, and let them love me created a barrier that left me more depressed, more suicidal, and more alone—no matter how widely I smiled or how kind I was to others.

I knew that if I wanted to stay alive and enjoy the world around me, I needed to start loving myself. As I began practicing self-love, I made some interesting discoveries.

I learned that loving myself means believing I am worthy of love and belonging. It means that I am willing to develop my talents and abilities, because I recognize that I have them and love myself for having them. Loving myself means that I am willing to be vulnerable and open, because I know I deserve all that I stand to gain from being vulnerable and open. And loving myself also means that I am willing to have boundaries and say no, because we naturally want to stand up for and protect the ones we love, ourselves included.

I am a licensed clinical social worker with over 25 years of mental health experience. I have been trained in emotionally focused couples therapy, trauma recovery, EMDR, neurolinguistic programming, psychodrama, and neuroscience. I have written a best-selling workbook, *Finding Peace*, which lays out a pattern of healing from attachment wounds. (I'll have much more to say about those shortly.) My mission is to bring greater love, light, and healing to the world.

Loving ourselves is not selfish. Loving ourselves is an essential element of being able to love others. Loving ourselves means that we have developed resiliency to the shadows of shame that whisper to us, *You are not enough.* Loving ourselves means that we can be authentically kind to others without a mask. We are not pretending or hustling, nor are we shutting people out. We are standing in our own light and sharing that with others. Loving ourselves means that we acknowledge we are not perfect, and we are gentle with ourselves. You are likely aware that we tend to be harder on ourselves than we are on anyone else. When we practice loving-kindness toward ourselves, a miracle happens: We stop being so judgmental of ourselves, and, in turn, we're also less judgmental of others.

Loving ourselves does not mean becoming conceited or vain. Loving ourselves does not mean we elevate our status above others or believe we are more important than others. Nor does it put us below others; we are not a burden or worth less. When we are not encumbered by the messages of doubt, shame, fear, and pretending, we are better able to connect with those around us. Loving ourselves allows us to show up in the world so we can love others, uplift others, and make the world a more loving place.

Throughout this book, there will be references to *attachment wounds* and the *shadows of shame.* My earlier *Finding Peace* workbook explores these topics in greater detail, but it is important to understand these definitions as you embark on your year of self-love. These attachment wounds fall into six main categories: loss, rejection, neglect, betrayal, abandonment, and abuse. We are wired to connect with others, yet there are times when those connections are severed or damaged, causing us a great deal of pain. There are also times when we exacerbate these wounds ourselves. We end up rejecting ourselves, neglecting our needs, betraying who we really are, and sometimes even abandoning or abusing ourselves.

Love and connection are the only ways I have found to heal these wounds. This book gives you daily activities to practice loving yourself in order to become more accepting, reassuring, present, and compassionate with yourself, which will empower you to do the same with others.

If you have not been kind to yourself for a while, when you first try these activities you may find them challenging. Don't give up. You are likely to be bombarded by the shadows of shame, our negative core beliefs and messages personified. They are the internal dialogues running through our mind that enhance feelings of worthlessness and powerlessness, as well as a lack of emotional safety or trust. The shadows of shame demand perfection, perpetually proclaiming we are not enough. They whisper that we are powerless and weak; they discourage us from continuing to try. They tell us our needs are not as important as others' needs. They encourage us to put on a mask to hide how we feel about ourselves. Sometimes they urge us to engage in rebellious behaviors regardless of the consequences. All of this separates us from connection, love, and compassion.

The good news is that you are not your shadows. You are a being of light. You are worthy of love. And to help you stand in that light, this book gives you daily quotes, tips, activities, or meditations. You are worth the effort. If you feel like you are not succeeding, that's a perfect opportunity to practice loving yourself in that very moment.

May you find greater peace and love through this experience. May you discover the truth: You are worth loving.

JANUARY

1
JANUARY

~~~

It's a new year! Many people write down their New Year's resolutions with every intention of achieving them only to lose traction and hope within a few weeks, or even a few days.

I invite you to try something different this year. Set your intention. What is one thing that you would like to experience more of this year: joy, love, compassion, fitness, forgiveness, or happiness? Think of a word that encapsulates what you want to experience more of. Write it down. Write it on a mirror. Write it on social media. Even if you've added a small drop of that thing to your life by the end of the year, you will have made an improvement. That is success.

2
JANUARY

~~~

"Great things are not done by impulse, but by a series of small things brought together."

—VINCENT VAN GOGH

3

JANUARY

~~~

The tenets of self-love include:

- ❏ Courage
- ❏ Trust
- ❏ Resilience
- ❏ Growth
- ❏ Forgiveness

- ❏ Empathy
- ✔ Gratitude
- ❏ Nourishment
- ❏ Truth
- ❏ Mindful awareness

- ❏ Emotional intelligence
- ❏ Connection

Pick one of these principles and think about what it means to you.

4

JANUARY

~~~

Have some fun with this one. Treat yourself to a shopping excursion (to a stationery store or bookstore) and pick out a blank journal to guide you on your self-love journey. It can be a fancy one with a cover you love or a simple spiral-bound notebook. Use your journal as a way to track your progress. Writing down your experiences is a powerful way of learning more about yourself.

5

JANUARY

~~~

As you work on loving yourself, you may experience pain. You may be tempted to numb it. I invite you to instead look at these uncomfortable feelings with a different perspective; these are growing pains, like working out to build muscles.

6

JANUARY

~~~

Self-love is different from narcissism. When we love ourselves, we know that we matter, that we are worthy of love and kindness, and that it is OK to be kind to ourselves. Then we can be more present and loving to others.

7
JANESRY

～～～

Like a caterpillar going through the mysterious process of metamorphosing into a butterfly, you may be wrapped in a chrysalis of shadows, wounds, and numbing behaviors. You may think it would be wonderful to have someone open your chrysalis and pull it away to free you. But like a butterfly, you must grow beyond the chrysalis's confines and break through its layers on your own.

What are some of the layers of your chrysalis? Take a few minutes to journal about what they are, and then imagine how it will feel to shed them.

8
JANUARY

～～～

"The greatest homage we can pay to truth, is to use it."

—JAMES RUSSELL LOWELL

9
JANUARY

~~~

What are some kind things that you would love to have someone say to you? Take some time to think back and remember kind words that have made a difference to you in the past. Perhaps they boosted your spirits when you were down, or reminded you that you are loved. Look in the mirror and say a few of these messages to yourself. Notice how hearing these positive things makes you feel.

10
JANUARY

~~~

Some people find it hard to spend a few minutes on loving themselves. The shadows of shame whisper that it is selfish or that others need you. Give yourself permission to be loving with yourself. Write a permission slip to yourself and sign it.

11
JANUARY

~~~

I radiate love and light.

12
JANUARY

~~~

Imagine that you've won your dream car at a raffle. You are so excited to drive it around, but you notice that it is nearly out of fuel. Would you pull up to the local gas station and pour four liters of soda into the fuel tank? No? Why not?

Our bodies are amazingly designed. If we fill them with junk, how does that affect our performance? Feeding your body with the proper fuel is one way of loving yourself that can have lifelong benefits. What can you eat today that can fuel your brain, heart, and body? Think of fresh, whole foods that can give you both pleasure and a lasting feeling of satisfaction.

13
JANUARY

~~~

Educator and author John Bradshaw once said, "We give time to the things we love." Consider how much time and attention we put into the people we love and the hobbies we enjoy. If we give very little time and attention to a loved one, this conveys the message that they are not worthy of our time. Think about how much time you invest in your own self-care. How can you send yourself a clearer message that you are worth your time and attention?

14
JANUARY

~~~

The loudest shadow of shame is the critical voice in your head who scolds: *Why did you do that? You should be doing this. You look horrible in that. You are too fat. You are too skinny. You didn't try hard enough.* Can you hear it? Take a moment and imagine what that voice sounds like. Imagine what this judge looks like.

Today, notice how often the judge shows up. Every time, practice the mantra: *I see you. I don't believe you. I am learning to love myself.*

15
JANUARY

~

"Remember, you have been criticizing yourself for years and it hasn't worked. Try approving of yourself and see what happens."

—LOUISE HAY, *YOU CAN HEAL YOUR LIFE*

16
JANUARY

~

The shadows of shame lie to us. One powerful way to find freedom from the shadows is to tell the truth. When the shadows berate you over a mistake, examine the facts (the things you can see, hear, touch, smell, or taste) without a judgmental commentary.

Once you have identified the facts of a situation, you can make a more educated decision about how to handle it. You have the power to counter those lies with facts.

Look out for the lies and start telling the truth.

17
JANUARY

~~~

Self-love is not selfish. It is generous, creating an overflow of love that spills out around you, touching family, friends, and strangers. Loving yourself gives you more love to share.

18
JANUARY

~~~

Is there something you have been putting off because it feels too uncomfortable? Lean into the discomfort and connect with your inner strength. Take a leap of faith in yourself and take action. See what happens.

19
JANUARY

~

**"Go placidly amid the noise
and the haste, and remember what
peace there may be in silence."**

—MAX EHRMANN, *DESIDERATA*

20
JANUARY

~

May I be kind
to myself.

21
JANUARY
~

One of the ways you can nourish your body and mind is through the element of water. Practice loving yourself by drinking water today. It cleanses, enlivens, and enriches your body. And you don't have to spend an extra penny; most bottled water is simply tap water, the same water that flows from faucets and drinking fountains.

22
JANUARY
~

Put both hands on your midriff, right between your belly button and your sternum. The tips of your middle fingers should barely touch at the midpoint. Now, take a deep breath. Imagine that you are filling up a balloon in your stomach. As you breathe, notice that your fingers pull slightly apart. Slowly let out the air and notice how your fingers come back together. When you breathe deeply like this, your brain gets the signal that all is right in the world, and you begin to relax. Practice breathing like this several times today.

23
JANUARY

~~~

Instead of looking at the ground, look up. Look at the sky. Notice the colors. Notice the clouds. Breathe in the beauty. Imagine that the universe is smiling down on you. What positive message is the universe trying to tell you?

24
JANUARY

~~~

When you notice you are suffering, acknowledge it. Acknowledging your suffering does not make you weak. In fact, it gives you more options to choose how you want to respond. When you feel this pain, acknowledge that it hurts; then do an act of kindness to yourself. Give yourself a hug, put a warming or cooling hand on your face, or rub your neck and shoulders. You may be suffering, but you also have the power to heal.

25

Have you heard of a vision board? The concept is simple. Go online and do an image search for the kind of experiences, feelings, or goals you would like to work toward. Print these images, cut them out, and paste them on large poster paper. Post the board where you can see it every day. As you look at it, ask yourself: *What is one small thing I can do today that will bring me one step closer to experiencing any of the things on my poster?*

26

Do you like sleeping in? Try this the next time you are going to get out of bed. Before you swing your feet over the side of the bed and sit up, just breathe. Close your eyes and feel the sheets with your feet. Notice the texture and temperature. Be mindful of this simple pleasure of being able to lie in bed for a moment longer.

27
JANURY

~

By learning to love and treasure myself, I will become that much better able to deeply love and treasure someone else.

28
JANUARY

~

Throughout the day, practice mindfulness. Notice how you are sitting in your chair: the sensation of your weight being supported. Notice your breathing: the steady rhythm, how it changes with emotions and activity. Notice the sounds around you, from the faintest whisper that you had tuned out to loudness that makes you cover your ears. Notice the colors, the sights, the people, and the textures. Give yourself permission to stop time for a moment and just be here and now.

29
JANURY

〜

"No man can produce great things who is not thoroughly sincere in dealing with himself."

—JAMES RUSSELL LOWELL

30
JANUARY

〜

Is there something you've wanted to achieve, but it feels too daunting to even begin? Write down a reason that you feel like you can't accomplish it. Is this statement 100 percent true? Below that reason, write down three of your strengths that will help you as you pursue this goal.

low self-esteem

I have a lot going in me.

31
JANUARY

~~~

Thoughts inspire us to create, build, and take action. They can also destroy, harm, or disempower. If we want to experience more positive emotions or more love, we will need to change our thoughts. What thoughts permeate your mind? Which ones serve you well, and which ones hold you back?

Today, try to act on every thought of generosity, love, and positivity that comes to you. See what happens.

FEBRUARY

1
FEBRUARY

~~~

Laughing can soothe tension, relieve your stress response, boost your immune system, help you feel happier, and act as a natural pain reliever. Do yourself a favor and start laughing. If you need help getting started, watch a funny video or a stand-up comedy routine. Once you start, you might find it hard to stop.

2
FEBRUARY

~~~

Self-love is self-discipline. When we love ourselves, we are willing to discipline ourselves to support our growth. Loving yourself is as much about saying no to distractions and time wasters as it is about saying yes to good opportunities.

3

~

Get out a sheet of paper, set a timer for five minutes, and start writing a list of all the things you have accomplished in your life. No need to make it fancy or organized like a resume; just write down whatever comes to mind and keep going until the timer stops. The accomplishments can be big or small. When you think you're finished, reset the timer for 10 minutes and read through your list, recalling those times in your life. If this stirs up memories that remind you of other accomplishments, add them to the list. Now read through your final version and celebrate all the things you have done. Realize that you are amazing!

4

~

Consider some of the things that you do, perhaps without thinking, that subtract from the value of your day. Make a list. Can you set a boundary that will prevent one of these actions from contributing negatively to your life? Maybe you can say no to doing someone a favor that you really don't have time for.

This may feel uncomfortable, but you are making an important choice for yourself.

5

Have the courage to ask for help.
If you are in search of validation,
comfort, or reassurance, you can ask
someone to meet that need for you.

6

Choose a daily habit you would like to improve. At the end of each day, check off whether you did it or not. Celebrate when you succeed, but be kind to yourself when you don't. It takes weeks or months for a change like this to settle in. Tomorrow is a new day and you get to try again.

7

FEBRUARY

~~~

Expressing joy can make you feel more vulnerable than expressing any other emotion. You can show your joy through a laugh, a cheer, or a hug of celebration. Give yourself permission to express joy today.

8

FEBRUARY

~~~

Value your body today. Take some time to move around or exercise, even if for only a few minutes. Take the stairs, pull a few weeds, or empty your recycling basket. Notice your strength and appreciate all your body can do for you.

9

~~~

Part of loving yourself is learning to identify your emotions. When we've gotten out of touch with our emotions, or learned to suppress them, we don't recognize why our body is feeling pain or discomfort. But we can learn to trace those feelings to the source.

To gain this skill, try the Movie Exercise. When you have some private time, watch a movie clip that you know will be sad, scary, or anger inducing. Now close your eyes. If you can, name the emotion, and then describe where and how you are feeling it in your body. For example: *I am feeling sadness. I am feeling heaviness in my stomach and burning around my eyes.*

By taking a few minutes to do this exercise in a safe environment, you can train yourself to be mindful of the physical sensations that accompany your emotions. The next time you feel these sensations, look for a cause of sadness, fear, or anger. Notice whether this helps you understand your responses and take action to remedy the cause of your emotions.

10

FEBRUARY

~~~

Congratulate yourself on practicing self-love. Every day, you are making a choice to show up for yourself, and that is something to be celebrated.

11

FEBRUARY

~~~

Remember, you are a small piece of the world, but that does not mean you are insignificant. When you express loving-kindness to another person, with a simple gesture of caring or generosity, it reminds them that they are worthy of love, too. The ripples from that small act can spread far, connecting you with something greater than yourself. What small loving act can you offer today?

12

FEBRUARY

~~~

"Whether or not it is clear to you, no doubt the universe is unfolding as it should."

—MAX EHRMANN, *DESIDERATA*

13

~~~

You are not perfect. (None of us are.) Sometimes you make mistakes. (All of us do!) But you are *you*. There is no one else in the world quite like you, and no one else brings to the world what you bring. You learn from your mistakes. Your imperfections create character. And you are enough.

14

~~~

Imagine finding a lost pet on the side of the road. The animal is dirty, hungry, and alone. Would you drive by, hoping someone else will take care of the animal? Or would you stop and help? What are the characteristics of a person who is willing to stop what they are doing to help an animal in need?

Write down the characteristics of this type of person. You have the capacity to embody all of these attributes, not just in relation to this hypothetical animal, but also in relation to others and to yourself. Think about the ways you can put these characteristics into action.

15
FEBRUARY

~~~

When was the last time you took yourself out on a date? Get your calendar out and schedule a date with yourself. Maybe you will spend time in nature, get a soothing, restorative massage, or immerse yourself in a hobby. Pick something that will be enjoyable, relaxing, or uplifting.

16
FEBRUARY

~~~

What makes you thrive and feel alive? Take five minutes to journal about your answer.

17
FEBRUARY

~~~

There are four categories in which we can do something daily to enhance our well-being: Fitness, Family, Friends, and Focus. Fitness means taking care of your body, and that's much more than working out at a gym. Hiking, dancing, gardening, playing fetch with your dog—there are unlimited self-loving ways to give your body the movement it craves. Family and Friends refer to making daily connections with your loved ones, whether it's a shared routine or a special gathering. Lastly, Focus refers to doing something daily to accomplish your personal mission. Think about each of these categories. Which ones do you already benefit from doing daily? Is there one (or more) that could use some loving attention from you?

18
FEBRUARY

~~~

Sometimes we can be hard on ourselves. We call ourselves names, we lament our body's limitations, and we put ourselves down with hurtful words. Sounds like bullying, doesn't it? Bullies often are like that because deep inside, they are wounded people. Chances are, if you are bullying yourself, you have some underlying wounds that need care and love. So today, turn the tables on your inner bully. Say something nice to yourself instead.

19

"Until you make the unconscious conscious, it will direct your life and you will call it fate."

—CARL JUNG

20

Get out a notebook and write down something you are anxious about. Write for as long as you want. When you are done, close the book and go do something else. Don't pick up the book for a day or two. After you have waited a few days, read what you wrote. Notice how you feel now. Has anything shifted?

21
FEBRUARY

Positive thoughts are some of the most powerful tools in your self-love journey. Use them today; every time you feel yourself drifting toward the negative, pull your mind back to the positive. It may be hard, but you have the strength to make this change.

22
FEBRUARY

Meditate on what your life can be like if you believe 100 percent you are worthy of love and belonging. How much will you allow people to love you? How much will you be able to love others?

23
FEBRUARY

〜〜〜

"After two decades of research on shame, authenticity, and belonging, I'm convinced that loving ourselves is the most difficult and courageous thing we'll ever do."

—BRENÉ BROWN, "THE MIDLIFE UNRAVELING"

24
FEBRUARY

〜〜〜

All I need is what is within my reach. I live in the midst of great abundance.

25
FEBRUARY

~~~

Think about a time in your life when you were vulnerable and journal about it. Even though it was probably difficult, chances are that through experiencing this vulnerability you also grew. Chances are you learned something about yourself. What did you learn? How have you become stronger as a result?

26
FEBRUARY

~~~

A powerful way to shift your thoughts and feelings is to talk or write to yourself in the second person. For example, instead of saying to yourself, *I can do this; I have been practicing all week,* you say, *(Insert your name), you can do this; you have been practicing all week.* Strangely enough, this simple shift into the second person can boost your mood and help you feel happier and more positive, making you more likely to accomplish your goals.

27
FEBRUARY

~

"Always do right.
This will gratify some people
and astonish the rest."

—ORIGIN UNKNOWN; ATTRIBUTED
TO MARK TWAIN AND LEO TOLSTOY

28
FEBRUARY

~

We make better choices for our bodies and our lives when we are grounded in love and compassion. Approach the world with compassion, be kind to yourself, and give yourself permission to feel and express your emotions. You will feel the difference in your body.

MARCH

♥

1

MARCH

~

"Failure is the opportunity to begin again more intelligently."

—HENRY FORD

2

MARCH

~

We are working on growing, changing, and becoming. Sometimes the distance we need to travel seems impossibly far. Think about your journey as an ultramarathon. Instead of standing at the starting line thinking, *I am going to run a hundred miles today*, calculate the time it will take you to reach the first aid station, and then the next. There are people all along the way who will encourage you, nourish you, and attend to you if you fall. All you need to do is take it a few miles at a time.

3
MARCH

~

The shadows of shame can convince you that you need to pretend in order to receive validation from others. But any validation you end up receiving is bittersweet. Although it feels good, it doesn't feel real, because you haven't been your true self.

Consider the ways in which the shadows of shame encourage you to be fake. What would it be like to take off the mask and let others see you as you are?

4
MARCH

~

"A human being . . . experiences himself, his thoughts and feeling as something separated from the rest, a kind of optical delusion of his consciousness. This delusion is a kind of prison for us, restricting us to our personal desires and to affection for a few persons nearest to us. Our task must be to free ourselves from this prison by widening our circle of compassion to embrace all living creatures and the whole of nature in its beauty."

—ALBERT EINSTEIN

5
MARCH

～～

"I love you. I'm sorry. Please forgive me. Thank you." This is the ancient Hawaiian practice of forgiveness known as Ho'oponopono. It can open our hearts to more love. Repeat these words and release any negative energy trapped in your body.

6
MARCH

～～

"'Enough' is a feast."

—BUDDHIST PROVERB

7
MARCH

~~~

As part of loving yourself, pay attention to the stories you tell yourself. Practice identifying your thoughts: Is this thought true, or is it just a warped or inaccurate story you are telling yourself? Take a moment to check the validity of the story. Sometimes sharing a thought with another person can help you identify whether it's accurate. Whether you are checking in with yourself or someone else, start getting in the habit of challenging these inaccurate stories.

8
MARCH

~~~

Think of a time when someone was kind to you for no particular reason, just because. Can you remember what the person said or their tone of voice? What emotions did the person show? Did they touch you in a gentle or compassionate way? How do you feel as you remember this moment?

9
MARCH

"Be merciful. If it is a mess, let it be a mess. If it feels like you can't do this today, stay put and explore that feeling . . . Be a work in progress while holding this blueprint. The feeling of its being difficult is actually the sensation of your life evolving. Embrace it."

—RALPH DE LA ROSA, *THE MONKEY IS THE MESSENGER*

10
MARCH

Visit a restaurant you have never been to before, or try a new food you have never eaten. Maybe you will find that you like it; you've expanded your palate and opened yourself up to new choices and discoveries. Maybe you will find that you didn't like it, so no need to try it again. Either way, you will have learned something new about yourself.

11
MARCH

"Shared sorrow is
half sorrow, shared joy
is double joy."

—UNKNOWN

12
MARCH

You can build your brain power the same way you strengthen your muscles.
The more you engage your brain, the more it grows and changes. Sign up for
that language class you have always been thinking about taking, pick up a
puzzle and solve it, read about a new topic; whatever you choose, do something
to build your brain today.

13
MARCH

~~~

Many of us are terrified of being rejected because of experiences in our past. We navigate around rejection because the idea of opening that wound scares us. But fear of rejection can hold us back; it stops us from taking risks and being vulnerable, even when we might benefit from doing so.

So try this. Think of a favor or a service you can ask someone for that you are almost certain will result in a no. It could be something as small as requesting more food at a restaurant or asking a stranger for a hug. You will hear no, and you will be OK. Teaching yourself how to live with rejection is an important step in opening yourself up to new experiences with unpredictable outcomes.

14
MARCH

~~~

I trust my intuition and inner voice.

15
MARCH

~~~

Reach out to someone new today. It could be a friend or family member you haven't spent time with in a while, or a coworker you'd like to get to know better. Look for people with positive energy and surround yourself with them. Notice how you feel when you make a new connection or strengthen an old one. Realize that the person you've connected with is enjoying that feeling, too.

16
MARCH

~~~

Think about an aspect of yourself you have a hard time accepting. It can be a physical characteristic, a behavior, or a personality trait that you have struggled with. Journal about the emotions and thoughts you have about that issue. Practice awareness as you do so. Examine whether you feel drawn to bully yourself or to be kind. Just notice.

17
MARCH

~

"Have enough courage to trust love one more time and always one more time."

—MAYA ANGELOU

18
MARCH

~

Today, if you find yourself starting to get irritated with someone, become curious. Notice what is happening in your body. Say to yourself: *Isn't this interesting?* And then, with curious inquiry, step away from yourself and take a look at what is going on inside of you. Notice the sensations, the thoughts, and the emotions without taking it personally that the person behaved in this way. This process doesn't have to take a long time. But even for a few seconds, become curious with yourself. You may find that in the process you become more peaceful and grounded.

19
MARCH

~~~

I believe in the essence of who I am and what I was born to do.

20
MARCH

~~~

Be your own DJ and play your favorite songs. Sing out loud with the melody, or find a harmony. Dance or move to the rhythm of the beat. Close your eyes and experience what colors or memories show up as you listen to the music.

21
MARCH

~

All of us have wounds: wounds of rejection, loss, neglect, abandonment, betrayal, or abuse. Show yourself love by focusing on healing your wounds. The first step is becoming aware of them. The next step is to reach out and ask for help. A trusted friend, a family member, or even a stranger who's a wise and compassionate listener can be the remedy you need to help you heal.

22
MARCH

~

"The weak can never forgive. Forgiveness is the attribute of the strong."

—MAHATMA GANDHI, *ALL MEN ARE BROTHERS: AUTOBIOGRAPHICAL REFLECTIONS*

23
MARCH

~~~

If you catch your shadows of shame saying something negative to you,
write down at least *five* positive comments to counteract the negative thought.

24
MARCH

~~~

"The most beautiful people we have known are those who have
known defeat, known suffering, known struggle, known loss,
and have found their way out of the depths. These persons have
an appreciation, a sensitivity, and an understanding of life that
fills them with compassion, gentleness, and a deep loving concern.
Beautiful people do not just happen."

—ELISABETH KÜBLER-ROSS

25
MARCH

~~~

Healing happens faster when there is an environment of love, support, and connection. Think about the progress, accomplishments, and successes you've experienced recently. Make an effort to celebrate them, not just on your own, but with someone (or a few people) in your life.

26
MARCH

~~~

Dare to be present. There are so many ways to zone out and numb ourselves. Yet every day offers us regular opportunities to pay attention to the wonders of our world. Make a point of noticing the sunrise or the sunset. Step out into the rain and wind. Really experience a good deep breath. Stop and savor your food. Enjoy the warm smoothness of your own skin.

27
MARCH

~~~

Instead of promising yourself, *I will never do this again,* ask yourself, *What would help me do something else instead?*

28
MARCH

~~~

"If you do not forgive yourself, the shame you carry will compel you to continue to act in harmful ways toward others and yourself."

—BEVERLY ENGEL

29
MARCH

~~~

Give yourself a compliment. Focus on the progress you have made,
your willingness to stick to a goal, or how you solved a problem recently.
Notice how it feels to praise yourself in this specific way.

30
MARCH

~~~

"The least of things with
a meaning is worth more
in life than the greatest
of things without it."

—CARL JUNG

31
MARCH

~~~

How well do you know what brings you joy? When was the last time you explored your inner world? Spend some time today journaling about these prompts:

Some of my favorite memories are . . .

One of my dreams is . . .

One of the most challenging parts of my life has been . . .

My closest friends and family are . . .

What I love most about life is . . .

After journaling, think of someone with whom you would consider sharing some of what you wrote and reaching out to talk with them.

APRIL

♥

1
APRIL

I choose to smile today.
Smiles are contagious.
My smiles spread like ripples.

2
APRIL

**"He is a wise man who does not grieve
for the things which he has not,
but rejoices for those which he has."**

—EPICTETUS

3
APRIL

In the Harry Potter series, most of the wizarding world is so afraid of the evil Lord Voldemort that they will only refer to him as "He who must not be named." However, Harry Potter's mentor, Dumbledore, believes in calling things by their real names. This demystifies the shadowy title and decreases its power.

Naming our emotions does the same thing. When we can verbally acknowledge what we are feeling, it is the first step in facing our fears and choosing how we will react to the emotion.

4
APRIL

Imagine that you needed heart surgery. You might look for a surgeon who has a calm bedside manner, or is kind or encouraging. At the same time, you will want a surgeon who actually knows how to do open heart surgery, a doctor with a lot of experience and practice, who can solve problems if they arise.

Does your emotional heart need reconstructing? You are the best person to do emotional heart repair. It will help if you have both a compassionate temperament and the ability to behave compassionately through skilled actions. Where are your strengths? Can you take small steps to improve in both categories?

5
APRIL

~~~

Think of a part of yourself you are having a hard time loving. It could be a part of your body, a behavior, or anything else you don't really like. Write down the negative messages you tend to tell yourself. Only write a sentence or two.

Now close your eyes. Imagine a being who loves you unconditionally. This could be a friend, family member, someone living or dead, or even someone imaginary. This being knows you better than anyone else and accepts you just the way you are. This being is loving, kind, and compassionate.

Write a letter to yourself from this person. What would this loving, kind, and accepting person say to you about the issue you identified? Write the letter with as much graciousness and compassion as you can.

When you are done, put the letter away for a little while. Come back later and read it to yourself aloud. Notice how you feel.

6
APRIL

~~~

I am where I am supposed to be right now. Everything that has ever happened in my life has brought me to this place. Today, I have the chance to open up to a new possibility: a street I've never walked on, music I've never heard before.

7
APRIL

When you allow yourself to be seen and express your needs, you give yourself the chance to be seen, accepted, valued, and loved. You open yourself up to having your needs met.

8
APRIL

> "Go within every day
> and find the inner strength
> so that the world will not
> blow your candle out."

—KATHERINE DUNHAM

9
APALL

~

Peter Vidmar scored a perfect 10 at the 1984 Olympic games and took home one silver and two gold medals in gymnastics. His secret? Fifteen minutes. Most gymnasts practice every day for six hours. Peter decided that he would add just 15 minutes extra to his workout. It may not sound like much, but it adds up.

Think about some skills you've been trying to develop or goals that you've been trying to meet. This doesn't have to be Olympic gold. It could be music practice, yoga, or clearing out clutter in a drawer or a closet. Plan to devote 15 minutes a day to one goal, or mix it up throughout the week. Just 15 extra minutes a day adds up—that's nearly two hours each week. Imagine the possibilities!

10
APRIL

~

I embody love and compassion.

11
APRIL
~~~

Many people feel uncomfortable and self-conscious about their bodies. It can be challenging to sign up for a fitness class, register for a race, or even put on athletic shoes to go for a walk. At the same time, being willing to try something to take care of your physical body is a great way to love yourself. What can you do to step out of your comfort zone and care for your body?

12
APRIL
~~~

"When one door closes, another opens; but we often look so long and so regretfully upon the closed door that we do not see the one which has opened for us."

—ALEXANDER GRAHAM BELL

13

Hey, self, you took a chance yesterday. You were a little worried to try that, but it turned out OK, didn't it? What could you do today that would be another stretch, and might turn out even better?

14
APRIL

~~~

It's easier to love ourselves when we connect with others in real life. One of
the strangest revelations about all the social media we surround ourselves
with these days is that much of it actually increases loneliness and depression.
Seeing the highlights of our friends' and followers' lives makes it easy to compare
ourselves and feel that our own lives are coming up short. Take a break from
social media today. Instead, make a phone call, send an email, or even write
a good old-fashioned letter or card to someone you've lost touch with.
Share the love.

15
APRIL

~~~

"We should certainly count our blessings, but we should also make our blessings count."

—NEAL A. MAXWELL

16
APRIL
~

Were you ever given a seed to plant when you were a child? You placed some rich potting soil in a small paper cup and buried the seed. You waited to see what would happen. Your teacher probably told you that the seed would need water and sunlight in order to grow. And so, every day, you dutifully gave it a little water as it sat by the window. Days later, a small green leaf poked its way out of the soil and eventually grew into a plant that produced a flower.

Practicing self-love is like planting a seed of compassion in your own heart. It may be very small when you first plant it. There is excitement in wondering just how big a plant will grow from this seed. It will require patience and tender, daily care. Today, be sure to nurture the seed of compassion you have planted in your heart. Give it water and warm sunshine.

17
APRIL
~

Think of someone you are angry with. Try to think about them with compassion for a few minutes today. Wish them well on their journey. Notice how this makes you feel. How does this help you become more compassionate toward yourself?

18
APRIL

~~~

"Placing the blame or judgment
on someone else leaves you
powerless to change your
experience; taking responsibility
for your beliefs and judgments
gives you the power to change them."

—BYRON KATIE

19
APRIL

~~~

Tune in to your body right now. What are you feeling? Where are you experiencing that emotion in your body? What color is it? What temperature does it have? When else have you felt this way? What would you call this feeling? Getting into the practice of naming your feelings helps you become more aware of yourself. Give yourself permission to feel this emotion for a moment or two. Validate your feeling. And breathe.

20
APRIL

~

"Perhaps some of us have to go through dark and devious ways before we can find the river of peace or the highroad to the soul's destination."

—JOSEPH CAMPBELL, *THE HERO WITH A THOUSAND FACES*

21
APRIL

~

Love is our natural state of being. When we are in a place of compassion, kindness, and love (for ourselves and the world around us), we will be more at peace. We will more strongly enforce boundaries. We will show up with our light and power.

22
APRIL

Cameras can zoom in and focus on certain targets so that everything else fades into the background. We can do the same thing with our thoughts. If you catch yourself focusing on a negative thought, pay attention to the physical sensations in your body. Notice any tension, heat, or pain that rises to the surface.

Now shift your thoughts to something positive: the smell of rain in a garden, the rhythmic sound of waves breaking on a beach, petting a purring cat. Be as focused as you can be on the positive thought. Notice how your body changes as you shift focus. The things that we are not focused on fade into the background.

We have more power than we realize. The more we practice shifting our focus to positive thoughts, the more the negative fades into the distance.

23
APRIL

Many companies use team-building exercises to build trust. It's important to trust others, but also think about how you can apply this same idea of team building within yourself. Show appreciation for and trust in each part of your body, the way you would a coworker. As you recognize how the parts of your body work as a team, you'll naturally feel a greater respect for yourself.

24
APRIL

～

"You are a child of the universe,
no less than the trees and the stars;
you have a right to be here."

—MAX EHRMANN, *DESIDERATA*

25
APRIL

～

I am strong
in many ways.

26
APRIL

~~~

Everyone loves a hero story. In fact, most of the top box-office-winning movies tell stories about heroes. You have a hero story inside of you. You have conquered something or are perhaps facing a trial right now in your life.

Write down your hero story. Describe where your journey began and how you have chosen your route and your destination. How willing were you to embrace the journey at first? Recall and describe the friends and strangers who have helped you along the way. Think of the obstacles that you have overcome. What have you learned about yourself in the process? How have you changed and grown?

27
APRIL

~~~

Go to your local bookstore and find a book that looks interesting. If the store has a comfy chair, spend some time reading and relaxing. If not, find another calming place to nourish your mind.

28
APRIL

～～～

Today, tell yourself: *I am going to stand in my truth that I am enough. I am not going to run away or become overbearing. I am going to be me, in this moment, here and now.*

29
APRIL

～～～

"Be thankful for what you have; you'll end up having more. If you concentrate on what you don't have, you will never, ever have enough."

—OPRAH WINFREY

30
APRIL

~~~

When we feel the pain of an attachment wound, it is a signal that we are disconnected in some way. The antidote? Connection. It is an astounding development of our brain to help live, love, play, and support each other through the world. Today, be the one who reaches out to help, encourage, and support someone who needs connection, too.

MAY

1
MAY

I am a master mistake-maker. Each time I make a mistake, I figure out better ways to do things the next time.

2
MAY

Tonglen Meditation is one of the bravest forms of meditation you can practice. It is done by breathing in the suffering around us and breathing out love, joy, and kindness. It is challenging because we will have to confront our own attachment wounds and voices of self-doubt in the process. At the same time, it can be a powerfully healing practice.

Start out by getting into a comfortable position. When you are ready, tune into the suffering around you. It may be your own or that of someone you know.

Imagine the suffering has a color or energy. Breathe this into your body through your nose. As it enters your body, imagine that the energy shifts to love and compassion as if touched with a magic wand. Breathe out the compassion through your mouth.

Repeat the process, breathing in suffering, breathing out love and compassion.

Five minutes is a good start. Next time try for 10 minutes.

3
MAY

Consider a time when you were hurt through the actions of another. Close your eyes and ground yourself through mindful breathing. Imagine the person who hurt you, standing in front of you. See the human being in this person. Realize that this person has hopes, dreams, fears, and worries just as you do.

Perhaps the person has behaved in such a way that allowing them back into your life would be unsafe. You are not expected to invite such people back into your life. However, you can still practice compassion. Can you wish the person well on their journey? What message would you give to this person?

As you do this exercise, be mindful of your own thoughts, feelings, and shadows. When you are done, thank the person and say goodbye.

4
MAY

Share the best and worst part of your day with someone you love. Choose a time when you can both talk and listen without interruption. Ask them to share, too, and listen with full attention. Creating this dialogue deepens your understanding of what is going on in both of your lives.

5
MAY

〜〜

**"Let your mindfulness co-opt everything in your experience. . . .
Keep aligning with the intentions of your practice:
kindness, diligence, presence, attention, relaxation."**

—RALPH DE LA ROSA, *THE MONKEY IS THE MESSENGER*

6
MAY

〜〜

Forgiveness is about letting go of the resentment and anger that we have been carrying. It doesn't necessarily mean that we are granting a pardon or excusing a behavior. It simply means that we stop dwelling on an injury or injustice and nurturing a grievance. Consider off-loading those painful feelings that have been weighing you down.

7

MAY

Sleep is one of the most important ways to give your body and mind the support they need. If you are having trouble sleeping, you don't have to just toss and turn. There are all kinds of nonprescription tips and habits you can try to get a better night's sleep. Take time to wind down at the end of the day, keep electronics out of the bedroom, and make sure it's dark and quiet (use earplugs, if you need to). Keep the temperature a bit cool, if possible, with layers of covers you can adjust to just the right amount of comfort. Care for yourself by ensuring you get the best night's sleep possible.

8

MAY

Sometimes your body knows what you are feeling before your brain does. If you're not sure what you're feeling in a given moment, check in with your body. What is happening in your neck, shoulders, hands, chest, stomach, bowels, and legs? Just noticing these body sensations and giving yourself permission to feel them can help you name the emotion you are experiencing. What are you feeling now?

9
MAY

"The belief that unhappiness is selfless and happiness is selfish is misguided. It's more selfless to act happy. It takes energy, generosity, and discipline to be unfailingly lighthearted, yet everyone takes the happy person for granted . . . And because happiness seems unforced, that person usually gets no credit."

—GRETCHEN RUBIN, *THE HAPPINESS PROJECT*

10
MAY

A morning self-care routine creates balance and purpose. Some common practices are spending time reading a good book, practicing meditation, engaging in fitness activities, or journaling. It's a form of self-love that refreshes and inspires us for the rest of the day. Do you have a morning ritual?

11
MAY

~~~

I am whole, I am creative; I am me.

12
MAY

~~~

Pain and suffering exist in the world, but there is also love, compassion, and peace. It is part of the yin and yang. We don't fully appreciate the love, joy, and peacefulness of the world if we haven't experienced pain.

It would be wonderful to live without pain, but pain can be a helpful signal. When we accidentally touch a hot stove, pain immediately signals us to pull away. Our body does this reflexively; there is no decision-making involved. Emotional pain functions in much the same way, but when we experience painful emotions, we don't always recognize that it is time to make a change. Is there a hot stove in your life that you need to pull away from?

13
MAY

~~~

When you make a mistake, how willing are you to give yourself the benefit of the doubt? What about when your friend or coworker makes a mistake?

Many people are more willing to excuse their own mistakes because they understand their own intentions, even if their actions didn't have the desired result. But if we are having trouble loving ourselves, we may actually be harder on ourselves than we would be on a peer.

When you or someone around you makes a mistake, pay attention to your reaction. If you find yourself reacting with anger, try to practice compassion.

14
MAY

~~~

Imagine a museum where rare paintings are put on display. How does the museum care for these priceless items? What security measures are put in place? What technology protects them from harmful elements?

Like this art, you are so rare that there is no one else on earth exactly like you. Your value is immeasurable. Think about how you care for yourself. What boundaries do you put in place? Keep your unique, wonderful self protected and secure.

15
MAY
~~~

The shadows of shame often attack and berate us. We are so accustomed to having these negative judgments in our heads that we don't stop to consider whether they are fair or accurate.

   The next time you notice these shadows, imagine they are saying those hurtful things about someone you love. Tune in to how it makes you feel.

   Most likely, you are frustrated to see the pain that the shadows of shame are inflicting on your loved one. You probably want to stand up, intervene, and let the messenger know that you won't let them attack your loved one. You can do the same when shadows of shame are directed at you.

16
MAY
~~~

When you're lying in bed at night, take 10 minutes to think of all the things for which you are grateful. Start with your body. Go through all the parts of your body and marvel at their service to you. Then expand from there. What people are you grateful for? What comforts do you have in your life?

17
MAY

~

"A failure is not always a mistake,
it may simply be the best one can
do under the circumstances.
The real mistake is to stop trying."

—B. F. SKINNER

18
MAY

~

Often, when we find ourselves complaining about someone we don't like,
it is because we recognize qualities in them that we dislike in ourselves.
Try to respond positively to one of these qualities in yourself. You can acknowledge
that it is an area you would like to change, but that you are working on. Or you
can evaluate whether this perceived weakness or flaw is as negative as you might
think. Meditate on this for a few minutes, and then think about the person you're
complaining about. Do you feel any differently toward them? Why or why not?

19
MAY

~~~

An amazing salesman had a goal to sell $1 million of product in one year. He believed his life would be complete when he achieved this target. On the day he accomplished it, there was a momentary celebration. He was so excited. But the joy only lasted for about a day before he felt let down.

While accomplishing our goals brings joy and is deserving of our celebration, lasting happiness is found along the journey, not just at the destination. As you pursue your goals, make sure you take time to appreciate the smaller victories and learning experiences along the way.

20
MAY

~~~

"Many people are alive but don't touch the miracle of being alive."

—THÍCH NHẤT HẠNH, *THE MIRACLE OF MINDFULNESS: AN INTRODUCTION TO THE PRACTICE OF MEDITATION*

21
MAY
~~~

Many of us try to avoid feeling anything, especially pain. So we numb the pain and end up feeling nothing. As you practice mindfulness today, notice times when you might be tempted to numb yourself. Loving yourself means being open to all your emotions. Embrace that vulnerability.

22
MAY
~~~

Our thoughts, negative or positive, affect our bodies, our interactions with others, and the space around us. Be aware of how you feel when you say a negative comment to yourself. Does it help you be happier? Does it motivate you to improve? Or does it discourage you further?

Today, write down something positive about yourself, and then read it and explore the emotions that come up. Compare this to how you feel when you tell yourself something negative. Write in your journal about the experience.

23
MAY

~

When Fred Rogers accepted the Lifetime Achievement Award for his work, he invited the audience to take 10 seconds to identify who had helped them become who they are. Then he set the timer on his watch for 10 seconds. Let's follow his request today. Spend 10 seconds thinking about who has helped you become the person you are.

24
MAY

~

Discover the wondrous power of meditation. Meditation helps us achieve a more grounded connection with all of the principles of self-love (courage, trust, resilience, growth, forgiveness, empathy, nourishment, truth, and connection). You may not be familiar with how to meditate. There are books, apps, and online videos and courses that teach meditation; you can probably find local meditation classes, too. Or simply take time to sit quietly in stillness, eyes open or closed, letting thoughts pass through your mind, following the rhythm of your breath. Meditation can be that basic.

25
MAY

I choose life.

26
MAY

Stepping out of our comfort zone is actually an act of self-love that allows us to grow and learn more about our own strengths and abilities. Today, challenge yourself to learn three new things about a stranger or an acquaintance. See if you can build your rapport with that person. Maybe you will even begin or deepen a friendship. Afterward, spend some time journaling about what you learned about yourself in the process.

27
MAY

Integrity is making sure your actions match your words regardless of whether anyone is watching. It becomes easier to love ourselves when our behaviors match our values and commitments. When these are out of alignment, it's an open invitation to the shadows of shame to show up and berate us. When we are in alignment, our energy flows more powerfully, our sense of confidence is stronger, and we are not afraid to let our light shine.

28
MAY

If you have an electronic device, you know that it will eventually lose power and need to be charged. We don't berate the device for running out of power or spend a lot of energy shaming the device when it is empty. Instead, we simply look for a place to plug the device in to recharge.

We are not always as kind to ourselves when we feel depleted. We often shame ourselves or become upset that we are "so needy." The truth is, we are only as needy as our unmet needs. So, if you are feeling empty today, view it from the perspective that you need power. Think of ways that you could recharge yourself today: a brisk walk, a nap, a nice foot rub, or a scalp massage.

29
MAY

~~~

"Altogether, the idea of meditation is not to create states of ecstasy or absorption, but to experience being."

—CHÖGYAM TRUNGPA

30
MAY

~~~

I love a challenge.

31
MAY

Resilience refers to our ability to recover after going through challenging, defeating, and sometimes even traumatic events. Think of resilience like the scene in a kung fu movie when one opponent is knocked on their back and then quickly springs back up again. The individual has had tremendous training to complete that action, both physically and mentally.

Where do you fall on the resiliency spectrum? Are you able to pop right back up, ready to go emotionally, physically, spiritually, and mentally? Or are you more on the other end of the spectrum, struggling with depression and anxiety after being knocked down? Regardless of where you are on the spectrum, you can become stronger.

As you begin your own resilience training, you'll find a few key practices helpful. Catch negative thoughts and counter or redirect them, nurture gratitude, and look for a purpose that can steady you through setbacks. Journal about where you are on the resiliency spectrum. As you do, be loving, patient, and compassionate with yourself. You're building your resilience, not putting it to the test.

JUNE

♥

1

JUNE

~~~

An important way to love yourself is to reach out and ask another person to meet your needs, whether it is a hug, a listening ear, feedback, or just an opportunity to hang out.

Perhaps you've had negative experiences reaching out to others, and that makes you hesitant to do so again. Today, practice vulnerability and try one more time.

2

JUNE

~~~

I am willing to risk being seen because I have value and much to offer this world.

3
JUNE

~

Vulnerability can't be forced. We can't expect people to open up and share what is going on inside if we have not created an environment of safety and support. Similarly, if someone asks us to share something personal, whether it is in a group or individually, and we don't feel safe sharing, it's perfectly all right to decline to answer. Self-love is about protection as much as it is about being open. If you want to draw closer to others, work on helping the relationship feel safe first. Ponder ways that you can help the relationships that matter the most to you feel safer.

4
JUNE

~

"Courage is found in unlikely places."

—J. R. R. TOLKIEN

5
JUNE

Sit comfortably with your feet on the floor, and rest the back of one hand in the palm of the other. Close your eyes, and breathe.

Now imagine loving yourself just as you are, unconditionally. Feel the warmth of that gentle, caring, compassionate love. You cherish and respect yourself as the precious being that you are. Your choices are influenced not by the shadows of shame, but by your own truth and empowerment. You are confident in your gifts and talents; you share them gladly with the world around you. Take all the time you need to truly feel your love for yourself and the changes that brings to your life.

6
JUNE

Humility is an essential ingredient in helping us practice self-love. It helps us recognize our own humanity along with the humanity of those around us.

Humility is different than shame. Shame tells us that we are unworthy of love and belonging. If we find ourselves becoming defensive, pulling away, or beating ourselves up, chances are high that we are trapped in shame instead of experiencing humility. Humility says that we are not perfect, but we are trying. Keep this in mind as you go through your day.

7
JUNE

There are many ways to practice gratitude. One is to write down three things you are thankful for and why. Write it in a notebook, on social media, on a napkin, or wherever you'd like. The "why" part is important because it will help you be more thoughtful and mindful about the things for which you are grateful. You may discover new ways to appreciate the people or experiences you have written down.

8
JUNE

Sri Chinmoy said, "Smile, smile, smile at your mind as often as possible. Your smiling will considerably reduce your mind's tearing tension." Smiling reduces the stress hormone cortisol and adrenaline, while boosting hormones of endorphins, serotonin, and oxytocin. Just for fun, keep a tally of your smiles today. Try to smile more than 50 times and see what happens. Smiling all by yourself counts, too, of course. If you smile at someone else, notice if they smile back; smiling can be contagious.

9
JUNE

~~~

One of the attributes of empathy is perspective taking: the willingness to look at what is happening from someone else's point of view and seeing how their truth could feel right to them, even if we disagree. Pay attention to your disagreements today, whether they are personal or professional. When you notice you are coming up against a difference of opinion, take a moment to consider the situation from the other person's point of view. Even if you don't come away in agreement with them, this may give you an insight into how to resolve the issue or make a compromise. When you use this exercise to solve a problem, notice how you feel about yourself.

10
JUNE

~~~

Self-love is not about taking selfies with the beauty filter on. Self-love is about self-respect and loving yourself, in all your quirky, unique, individual glory. Try capturing some moments and expressions that are really *you*.

11
JUNE

~~~

"It takes a great deal of bravery to stand up to our enemies, but just as much to stand up to our friends."

—J. K. ROWLING, *HARRY POTTER AND THE SORCERER'S* STONE

12
JUNE

~~~

Shift your thoughts away from shame. When you feel your mind starting to drift in that direction, gently redirect it. Acknowledge you are feeling shame and respond to yourself with kindness.

13
JUNE

~~~

Trustworthy people are authentic. What we see is who they really are; they don't pretend, and they aren't trying to be someone else.

Being authentic this way often feels risky. When we act as our true selves, we can be afraid that our opinions will be met with disagreement, or that our choices will be met with ridicule. But succumbing to this fear means letting our anxiety get the better of us. Pretending to be someone else can end up harming you (and has the potential to hurt others, too).

When we are real, we can be trusted. We can connect more strongly with those around us, and we don't feel the pressure of pretending to be someone we're not. It may not always go perfectly, but it's worth the risk.

14
JUNE

~~~

"The moment you doubt whether you can fly, you cease forever to be able to do it."

—J. M. BARRIE, *PETER PAN*

15

~~~

Life is full of challenges, small and large. It feels great to overcome a challenge, but we can learn just as much (if not more) from stumbling on a challenge or needing to concede defeat. Think of a time you tried to meet a challenge and, though it didn't work out, you managed to keep trying. What did you learn about yourself when you got up and tried again? How did you grow through that experience?

16

JUNE

~~~

If we lack competence in something, we can do something about it. We can sign up for a workshop, take a class at school, or ask a mentor to teach us. Think of something you want to learn or improve upon. Where could you go to learn more about it? Take a step today to improve your competence. Register for a class, find an online course, or ask a mentor to teach you.

17
JUNE

~~~

One of the thieves of joy is jealousy and comparison. When we see that a person has a bigger house than ours, or makes more money than us, drives a fancier vehicle, or has the body of a movie star, the shadows of shame will use that data as "evidence" that there is something wrong with us or that we are not enough. But is it true? How much joy do we lose when we get caught in that trap? What would you be able to accomplish in the time you spend comparing yourself to others?

18
JUNE

~~~

"There is a stubbornness about me that never can bear to be frightened at the will of others. My courage always rises at every attempt to intimidate me."

—JANE AUSTEN, *PRIDE AND PREJUDICE*

19
JUNE

Zen Buddhist master Thích Nhất Hạnh teaches the Four Mantras of True Presence that can help us all connect at a deeper level with our loved ones. They are:

Darling, I am here for you.

Darling, I know you are there.

Darling, I know you suffer.

Darling, I suffer. I am doing my best, but I need your help and understanding.

We can also say these simple, yet powerful, mantras to ourselves as we practice self-compassion. Imagine that you are having a conversation with yourself using these mantras. Try it now.

20
JUNE

I can let it go.

21
JUNE

~~~

The simple power of naming your feelings can significantly decrease emotional arousal. The next time you are feeling an intense emotion, whether it is anger, fear, joy, or sadness, say it out loud: "I am feeling . . ." Notice what happens to your body when you call out the emotion.

22
JUNE

~~~

The Dalai Lama describes compassion as sensitivity to the suffering of self and others with a deep wish and commitment to relieve the suffering. It is often our nature to withdraw from suffering. We don't want to feel it. But when one of our loved ones is hurting, we have a desire to help. We want to do something to relieve the suffering, even for a moment. We want to help because we love and are committed to that person.

Try to do the same for your own area of hurt. Make a commitment to yourself and help relieve your suffering by treating yourself with gentleness and compassion.

23
JUNE

I recognize that my life
is abundantly full. I see the
gifts I have been given,
and I give myself permission
to express gratitude for
all that I have.

24
JUNE

~~~

The Compassionate Colors exercise creates an energy field of compassion that you can take with you wherever you go. Start by breathing in and out in a relaxing rhythm. With every breath you take, allow yourself to become a little more comfortable and relaxed. When you are ready, think of a color that you associate with compassion or loving-kindness. It can be whatever color you wish.

Imagine that this color begins to form above your head like a cloud in the sky. Now imagine that it begins to settle around you like fog. Imagine breathing in the color and allowing it to flow throughout your body, reaching down to your toes, up through your head, and down through your fingers. Imagine the color flowing through you and surrounding you. Imagine this color has a strength that can protect you and empower you to be more compassionate and kind.

You have the power to surround yourself with this compassionate energy any time you realize you are treating yourself unkindly.

25
JUNE

~~~

Think of a time when you have overcome hardship or challenge. Step into your courage and share this story with another person. Take a risk. Be vulnerable.

26
JUNE

~~~

"Darkness cannot drive out
darkness; only light can do that.
Hate cannot drive out hate;
only love can do that."

—MARTIN LUTHER KING, JR.

27
JUNE

~~~

We never outgrow the need to be appreciated, accepted, reassured, attended to,
or seen. Acknowledging that these needs are nonnegotiable empowers us to stop
shaming ourselves for needing love and affection, and it encourages us to get the
need met in healthy ways. It shows bravery to take risks and ask for what we need.

28
JUNE

~

It's OK that I have needs. It's a way of knowing I am alive.

29
JUNE

~

If you want to shift your mind-set into believing that you can achieve, learn, and grow, notice just how often the shadows of shame show up with their defeatist lies of judgment and powerlessness.

Write down these messages on a sheet of paper. Look at what you've written, and then turn it over. Don't spend any more time ruminating on the messages. Instead, write the opposite message on the other side of the paper. Notice how it feels to read that. Notice whether the deceptive voices want to crawl from the other side of the paper and squash your positive message. Just notice. Which messages do you really want to believe? Which bring you love, joy, and hope?

30

JUNE

~~~

There is a part of our brains called the anterior cingulate cortex (ACC). It has a unique function of helping to regulate our emotions while also helping us make decisions. You can visualize it working like the gearshift of a car.

Imagine you have big plans with someone you adore. Just as you are getting ready to walk out the door, the phone rings and your loved one tells you something came up. They aren't able to go. If energy and blood is flowing smoothly into the ACC, your brain can shift gears fairly quickly. You may be upset, but you are able to adjust rather quickly and the emotion fades. But if the ACC is not working on all cylinders, your gear shifter is likely to get stuck. You may find yourself battling obsessive thoughts, feeling spikes of anxiety or anger, and having difficulty thinking clearly about what to do next.

You can strengthen your ACC simply by recognizing what you are feeling in your body and identifying the emotion that is accompanying it. Neuroscience research has shown that devoting as little as five minutes a day can make a positive difference. That's it. A little mindful meditation can help you strengthen the ACC. It can help you become more flexible in managing your emotions and smoothing out those ups and downs. Try it today.

JULY

1

"If you want others to be happy, practice compassion. If you want to be happy, practice compassion."

—DALAI LAMA

2

We want to protect ourselves from the pain of rejection, abuse, neglect, or any other attachment wound. We do it almost unconsciously. We build a wall, brick by brick, to protect ourselves from suffering, only to discover that we have erected a prison with only a small window looking out into the world.

When we discover our prison, it can feel overwhelming, but we can begin to dismantle it in very much the same way as it was built: brick by brick.

3
JULY

~~~

One of the most loving things you can do for yourself is build healthy connections with others. Who can you connect with today? It could be someone you've never met before. Today, stay open and on the lookout for friendly strangers. Remember that you, too, could be a friendly stranger for someone else seeking a healthy connection.

4
JULY

~~~

"Real courage is when you know you're licked before you begin, but you begin anyway and see it through no matter what."

—HARPER LEE, *TO KILL A MOCKINGBIRD*

5

JULY

~~~

We have all made mistakes in our lives, and some of them have been hurtful to the people we love the most. It is natural to be reminded of these mistakes, either by the person we've hurt, or just by our own thoughts. When this happens, it is easy to jump right into shame and self-criticism, which does nothing for your loved one or yourself.

The next time you find yourself dwelling on a past mistake, lean into the discomfort, take responsibility for your actions, and then ask if there is anything that the person needs right now that could provide some comfort or support. Sometimes the answer is no, and that's OK. But when it's yes, go for it!

The more you practice self-forgiveness, the easier it will be to remain present with the person you love.

6

JULY

~~~

When we start practicing self-compassion, it can feel foreign, uncomfortable, or even scary. It takes courage to start doing something new. It can feel so much more comfortable and safe to stay with the same patterns, even if we end up feeling stuck. Give yourself time to make changes, and as self-compassion starts to come more naturally to you, celebrate!

7
JULY

You are a Compassion Warrior. You are strengthening your skills of love, kindness, patience, and tenacity. You guard against the shadows of shame and stand in a place of light. You find a community of belonging. You practice boundaries. You surround yourself with a family that has a track record of making healthy decisions, who role model positive self-care. You are willing to lean into pain in order to grow. You have gifts that bless this world.

8
JULY

Emotional intelligence is the ability to identify, control, and share your emotions, while interacting with others with empathy, fairness, and confidence. Emotional intelligence is often as important as intellectual intelligence, if not more so.

As you develop your emotional intelligence, you'll become more keenly attuned to your feelings and have more control over them. This starts with identifying what you are feeling. The greater your emotional vocabulary, the easier it is to cultivate mastery over your emotions.

9
JULY

"True forgiveness is when
you can say, 'Thank you
for that experience.'"

—OPRAH WINFREY

10
JULY

Allowing ourselves to be vulnerable is like fishing. If a fisherman throws in his nets, there is a risk that he may not catch anything. He could wait all day without catching one fish. At the same time, there is also the chance that he could catch a whole boatload of fish. One never knows. But there is a 100 percent guarantee that he won't catch anything if he doesn't throw his nets into the water.

11
JULY

~~~

There's a common misconception that when you meditate, you must completely clear your mind of all thoughts. When people try to meditate with this false belief, they can easily become discouraged. They close their eyes and begin to meditate. Within seconds, thoughts seemingly come out of nowhere: *What's for dinner? Did I forget to turn in that assignment to my boss? I wonder what my best friend is up to?* As soon as they catch themselves having these thoughts, they think they're doing it wrong. Actually, they are doing it right.

In identifying the thought, they can shift their focus back to the meditation. Every time they shift the focus, they are actually creating neurological connections that enhance their ability to learn, create, and relax.

So, the next time you try meditation and a random thought shows up in your brain, celebrate by saying, "I'm doing it right," and then return to the meditation.

12
JULY

~~~

There are several apps and podcasts that provide guided meditations on self-love, such as Insight Timer. Find one and listen.

13
JULY

≈≈

"When we fully understand the brevity of life, its fleeting joys and unavoidable pains; when we accept the facts that all men and women are approaching an inevitable doom: the consciousness of it should make us more kindly and considerate of each other. This feeling should make men and women use their best efforts to help their fellow travelers on the road, to make the path brighter and easier as we journey on. It should bring a closer kinship, a better understanding, and a deeper sympathy for the wayfarers who must live a common life and die a common death."

—CLARENCE DARROW, *THE ESSENTIAL WORDS AND WRITINGS OF CLARENCE DARROW*

14
JULY

~

Western culture celebrates winning. Consider the number of reality shows that focus on a winner by slowly eliminating all of the other contestants. Winning has become a cultural expectation that pushes us to outperform everyone else.

It isn't the push to be better that is problematic. The problem is that we are not always going to win. We are going to make mistakes, and sometimes our best efforts land us flat on our faces. If we believe that we have to be better than everyone else, the shadows of shame pounce, reinforcing that we are not enough.

There is a powerful antidote to this winner/loser syndrome. Instead of competing with other people, focus on your own growth. Work on achieving your personal best. At the same time, build connections with others. When the judgment of who is better is eliminated, it is so much easier to build friendships.

15
JULY

~

"Fear is a natural reaction to moving closer to the truth."

—PEMA CHÖDRÖN, *WHEN THINGS FALL APART*

16
JULY

~

I lovingly stand up
for what I believe in.

17
JULY

~

Think of your level of trust with each person you know as a jar. Whenever that person acts dependably or goes above and beyond for you, beans are added to the jar. In time, the jar can fill up.

If there has been a betrayal in the relationship, it's like dumping all of the beans out of the jar. The person who betrayed the trust now has to behave in ways that rebuild the trust, one bean at a time. The more acts of integrity they perform, the more beans are replaced.

If you notice an important trust jar is low, it may be a good opportunity for a conversation with that person. It may also be a good time to check in with yourself. Having high expectations from your relationships does not make you needy or difficult; rather, holding others to a higher standard is an important part of loving yourself.

18
JULY
〜〜

Dark chocolate not only has nutritional benefits, providing triple the antioxidants of green tea and lowering cholesterol and blood pressure, but it also releases endorphins that help us feel happy. It contains a high source of tryptophan, the amino acid required for our brains to make serotonin, the neurotransmitter that helps us feel joy. So have some dark chocolate today and smile. You are doing something good for your body and your mind.

19
JULY
〜〜

When I fall, I get back up again because I am resilient.

20
JULY
~

"Piglet noticed that even though
he had a Very Small Heart,
it could hold a rather large
amount of Gratitude."

—A. A. MILNE, *WINNIE-THE-POOH*

21
JULY
~

It is not our struggles, our wounds, our burdens, or our challenges that hold us back from becoming our best selves. It is the absence of hope that we can do it. Sometimes it is easy for us to give up on ourselves because we have lost hope that we can improve. We may not have the ability to change what happened to us. But we always have the ability to hope, dream, and imagine.

22
JULY

～

Put one hand out in a cupping shape. Say to yourself: *I know who I am*. Repeat it a few times. Now, put out your other hand in a cupping shape and say: *I know who I am not*. Repeat that a few times as well. Now, put one cupped hand into the other and say: *And that's what makes me, me*.

23
JULY

～

Get out your journal and a timer. Set it for 15 minutes and begin writing about a difficult experience. It can be a trauma, a challenge, an upsetting memory, or anything that is usually hard for you to think about. When the timer goes off, stop. Close the book and come back the next day, writing about the same experience. Do this for four days. That's it. Try it and see what happens for you.

24
JULY

~

Knowing our purpose significantly increases feelings of joy and contentment. Ask yourself: *Is there a population, cause, or organization that I want to serve?* Research the place you've identified and find out how you can help.

25
JULY

~

When we feel trustworthy, it heightens our confidence to show up and be seen. At times we might be battling imposter syndrome, a common phenomenon that causes us to doubt ourselves and feel fake even when we have the skills necessary to accomplish the task at hand. One powerful way of combating imposter syndrome is to challenge our self-doubt and lack of confidence with the question: *Is it absolutely true?*

If there is even the slightest sliver of falsehood in your claim to being an imposter, you can get a wedge in there and bust that lie apart! Then you can ask: *What* is *true?* By identifying what is and is not true, you realign yourself with reality and are in a better place to stand with confidence and authenticity.

26
JULY

~~~

Imagine getting into a time machine and going back to visit your younger self. This is your chance to share everything you want your younger self to know and to show them love and compassion. With all you've learned through your years of experience, what words of encouragement would you offer?

27
JULY

~~~

Getting feedback is one of the most vulnerable situations we can experience. And it comes up in many circumstances: when we apply for jobs, when we take tests, when we try out for sports, even when we are swiping or scrolling through the latest social media relationship app. We struggle with a desire to become better at what we are doing while we are also afraid of being wounded by rejection. The irony is that we need feedback so that we can improve.

Practicing self-love, especially at times when our wounds are raw and painful, is essential to humbly, courageously getting back up and trying again. Ask yourself: *How can this feedback make me better?*

28
JULY

Write down a positive affirmation. Browse back or look ahead in this book and choose one that resonates with you today, find one online, or make up your own. Set an alert to remind you to say it out loud to yourself at least 10 times today.

29
JULY

A frustrated mother began scolding her four-year-old boy for repeatedly going to the corner of their block. "How many times have I told you not to go to the corner?" she yelled. Obviously, she was terrified that the child would get hurt.

The little one said, "You have told me many times, mama, but what's a corner?"

Immediately the mother's anger left, and she realized that she had not made sure that her little one understood her expectations.

When we don't understand something, others may act irritated with us because we don't seem to get it. Have the courage to ask for clarification.

30
JULY

When we make a mistake, we often hope that the other person will understand when we try to explain what happened. When someone else makes a mistake, notice how you feel. Do you react with compassion, or are you tempted to blame them? The tendency to punish often stems from our own shadows of shame, which punish us when we make a mistake. We so want others to be kind to us, but if we have a hard time being kind to ourselves, it's harder for us to treat them with compassion. The more that we practice self-love, the less critical and judgmental of others we will be.

31
JULY

"You think your pain and your heartbreak are unprecedented in the history of the world, but then you read. It was books that taught me that the things that tormented me most were the very things that connected me with all the people who were alive, who had ever been alive."

—JAMES BALDWIN

AUGUST

1

AUGUST

A young boy attended one of the earliest performances of *Peter Pan*. Afterward, he was asked what part of the play he loved the most: the pirates, the dog, or the children flying through the air? The boy answered that what he loved most about the play was ripping the program into little pieces and dropping the paper like snow from the balcony onto the people's heads below.

James Barrie, the author of the play, laughed when he heard the response. He didn't take it as a personal insult; most likely, he saw the similarities between this playful boy and the character Peter Pan.

You may be tempted to internalize people's criticism or disinterest in your work, or even their negative feedback about you as a person. As an act of self-compassion, however, you can challenge yourself to not take other's responses personally. Instead, choose to act from a place of compassion and love, for both yourself and the other person. Others' behavior says more about them than it does about you.

Today, make it a personal goal not to take anything personally.

2

AUGUST

~~~

"To love at all is to be vulnerable. Love anything, and your heart will certainly be wrung and possibly broken. If you want to make sure of keeping it intact, you must give your heart to no one, not even to an animal. Wrap it carefully round with hobbies and little luxuries; avoid all entanglements; lock it up safe in the casket or coffin of your selfishness. But in that casket—safe, dark, motionless, airless—it will change. It will not be broken; it will become unbreakable, impenetrable, irredeemable."

—C. S. LEWIS, *THE FOUR LOVES*

3
AUGUST

~~~

Ask not: *What is wrong with me?* Ask: *What is right with me and how can I strengthen those qualities?*

4
AUGUST

~~~

Can you think of one time that shame had a positive, lasting motivational effect on your self-improvement? Often, when the shadows of shame are hard on us, it's because we are trying to reach an objective and feel like we are failing. What would a wise, experienced, loving person say to you to encourage you to reach your goals?

Take a little time to think of the most encouraging, motivational message of truth you have heard or read. Write the message down and post it somewhere you can see it on a regular basis.

5
AUGUST

~

"Being empathic is a
complex, demanding, and
strong—yet also a subtle
and gentle—way of being."

—CARL ROGERS

6
AUGUST

~

Research has shown that even the slightest reminder that we are connected to others increases our compassionate behaviors. Wherever you go today, look around you. What do you see that reminds you that you are connected to others?

7
AUGUST

〜

"It's not that I'm so smart,
it's just that I stay with
problems longer."

—ALBERT EINSTEIN

8
AUGUST

〜

It's easy to stay focused on our attachment wounds. But as we obsess, we inadvertently fixate on the people who created the wounds. This fixation can perpetuate our suffering. We may even be caught in asking the unanswerable question: *Why did this happen to me?* Perhaps a better question would be: *How can this wound help me love more fiercely and see the beauty around me more clearly?*

9
AUGUST

~~~

Heliotropism is the scientific term for the attraction of living things to light. It is the phenomenon that causes flowers to face the sun as it crosses the sky.

We humans are also living beings that thrive in the light. We gravitate toward that which inspires hope, illuminates joy, and brightens love. As an act of self-love, embrace the heliotropic effect and turn toward something that brightens your day.

10
AUGUST

~~~

"Any person capable of angering you becomes your master."

—EPICTETUS

11
AUGUST

~~~

I let go of the need to be perfect.
I am patient with myself.

12
AUGUST

~~~

**"It is courage, courage, courage,
that raises the blood of life to crimson
splendor. Live bravely and present
a brave front to adversity."**

—HORACE

13
AUGUST

~

Athletes often rely on visualization; they imagine themselves in peak physical condition, winning the game, or completing a play. You can do the same thing. Imagine yourself as a kinder, more courageous person, and see how it changes your perspective.

Close your eyes and breathe slowly. Now imagine yourself standing in front of you. See this being as compassionate, kind, and loving. Imagine the sights, sounds, tastes, physical sensations, emotions, and even smells that this other you might experience. Try to create the vision as vividly as possible. When you are ready, step into this other you. Allow everything you imagined to become part of you. Breathe into this experience and complete this sentence: *I am now more* _____.

14
AUGUST

~

I'm aligning my behaviors with my values.

15
AUGUST
~~

Once we have learned how to be kinder to ourselves, we have made it easier to be empathetic toward others.

16
AUGUST
~~

We all have people who just rub us the wrong way—the ones who always manage to push our buttons. There may be times when you have to interact with one (or more) of these people. It is tempting to avoid, dismiss, or embarrass them. When we practice self-love, however, we can use these situations to learn more about ourselves. What attachment wounds are hurt when you interact with this person? It could be that when they are around you, it stirs up some of your negative core beliefs about yourself. Maybe this person reminds you of someone from your past. Or could it be that this person displays attributes you don't like in yourself?

Pondering these possibilities will help you paint a more accurate picture of what is going on in your relationship with this person. You may discover that you haven't been seeing them or yourself in the most honest, accurate light. When you see things from a different perspective, does it change your feelings about this person?

17
AUGUST

~~~

A singer with a beautiful voice often made time to perform mini concerts at local nursing homes. During one particular concert, a frail woman in the audience began singing along. That wasn't an unusual occurrence for the singer, but he noticed, as the song progressed, that many others in the audience began to weep. When the concert was over and he was shaking the hands of those present, one of the guests came up to give him a hug. The guest explained that she was the daughter of the woman who had started singing along with him. Her mother had had a stroke several years ago that disabled her ability to communicate with words. It was the first time that the daughter had heard her mother use words in years.

There is great power in music. The main reason movies and television shows have soundtracks is to heighten our emotional experience. Music can move us to feel all sorts of emotions including excitement, love, and joy. It is communal. It brings us together in ways that other team-building activities can't.

Use the power of music in your life today. Listen to music that enlivens, soothes, or inspires you. Let it move you.

18
AUGUST

~~~

Hope is an essential element of resiliency and self-love. Take some time to answer these questions in your journal: What do you hope for? Has there been a time in your life when you felt hopeless? Do you still feel that way? If not, what changed? How does hope help you become more resilient and loving?

19
AUGUST

~~~

Often, when a person begins to express a concern, a worry, a frustration, or another type of dilemma, we stop listening to what they are saying and immediately go into problem-solving mode. Our concern comes from a place of compassion, but it also conveys an unspoken message that we don't think the other person can figure things out, especially if they haven't asked for help. More likely, they just want someone to listen.

To take it a step further, we believe that if we don't solve the problem, it reflects negatively on us. We are trying to protect ourselves against being judged.

If someone starts to tell you something that they are unhappy about, notice whether you feel pressure to fix it for them. Stop formulating answers and solutions in your mind. Breathe. And then listen.

20
AUGUST

~~~

"I do not ask the wounded person how he feels, I myself become the wounded person."

—WALT WHITMAN, *SONG OF MYSELF*

21
AUGUST

~~~

Let's make a list. Write down some of your favorite qualities about yourself. What are some of your talents? What makes you uniquely you?

It may take some time to create a full list, so don't feel rushed. It's fine to come up with a few things, and then wait for reminders to add more qualities. Keep the list handy. Add to it whenever you recall the qualities you appreciate in yourself or discover new ones.

22
AUGUST

~~~

If you listen to children play, you may hear them use the phrases "Do-over!" or "Re-do!" An outcome in the game didn't happen the way they wanted, so they get the chance to try again.

When we are practicing self-compassion, there may be times when what comes out of our mouths is less than kind or loving. At those times, we, like the children at recess, can say to ourselves *do-over* and immediately respond the way we really meant to. We may not be able to change the past, but we can take as many do-overs as life permits until we have fully developed our ability to love, forgive, practice compassion, and achieve the outcomes we desire.

23
AUGUST

~~~

If a rattlesnake bites you, you could beat the rattlesnake to death, or you could attend to the wound. The more energy you use to attack the rattlesnake, the faster the poison will flow through your body. Similarly, if you are wounded by the actions of others, you have two choices: you can go after the person who hurt you, or you can attend to the wound and seek healing.

24
AUGUST

〜

Safety is a necessary part of being vulnerable. Not everyone has earned the privilege of hearing our stories. Have you ever encountered a stranger who unloads their entire life story on you without asking permission? It usually feels uncomfortable because the two of you haven't established safety first.

There are two basic situations in which it is safe to share our stories with others. First, I'll share my story with someone if I need their support. Second, I will share my story if I think that it will uplift or support the other person.

If the situation does not meet one of those criteria, then I don't share. It isn't that I am hiding, but my story is sacred, and not everyone has earned the right to hear it.

Who in your life could benefit from hearing your story? Think of people with whom you have established the safety that you need to be open and honest.

25
AUGUST

〜

"The real meditation is how you live your life."

—JON KABAT-ZINN

26
AUGUST

〜

Medical professionals are increasingly writing "park prescriptions" for their patients. These are prescriptions to go outside, breathe in fresh air and sunshine, and spend time enjoying the world unplugged. Being outside decreases stress, improves feelings of happiness, reduces anxiety, and is beneficial to your heart.

You don't need to go see the doctor to get your own park prescription; write one for yourself. Go for a hike, spend time in a garden, dance in the rain, or watch a sunset.

27
AUGUST

〜

Take a hike. Go exploring. Find a new place to experience and enjoy.

28

~~~~

Two artists attempted to carve something out of a massive pillar of marble weighing several tons. The first artist fumbled with the chisel, and a chunk of marble broke away. He thought the stone was ruined and abandoned the job. Another artist was commissioned, only to give up before even trying to complete the job. No other artist felt up to the task of finishing the work, and so for decades the marble was shoved into a corner of the stone yard, exposed to the elements.

One day a young man, not even 30 years old, was hired to complete the commission. As Michelangelo inspected the marble, he envisioned who was trapped inside. Slowly, methodically, he chipped the marble away. For two and a half years, he toiled until it was finished. One of the most recognizable works of art, *David*, was unveiled to the world.

It's easy to see ourselves as those earlier artists saw the pillar. They gazed upon the broken marble: imperfect, ruined, abandoned. They felt too daunted by the challenge to take it on. They couldn't see what Michelangelo saw, waiting to be patiently uncovered, shaped, and polished.

Like that block of marble, you have amazing potential. You're a priceless work of art, just waiting to be revealed.

29
AUGUST

~

Dopamine is a powerful and essential neurotransmitter in our brain. It helps us feel pleasure and joy. When we have higher levels of dopamine, we learn faster, retain information better, and make wiser decisions.

We can boost our dopamine levels by doing random acts of kindness. Today, look for an opportunity to do something nice for someone else. Make it a secret mission; do your best to complete your act of kindness undetected. Afterward, take a few minutes to journal how doing a random act of kindness made you feel. Think about how the act is not only a blessing for someone else, but a form of self-love.

30
AUGUST

~

What decision have I been putting off making that my gut tells me I need to make today?

31
AUGUST

~~~

Mantras are one of the most common tools used to facilitate meditation; they are used throughout the world in many cultures, languages, and traditions. *Mantra* is a Sanskrit word meaning "a mind tool" or "mind vehicle." It is a word, sound, or phrase that we can use to clear the mind and calm the body. A mantra helps us focus our transient and scattered thoughts onto one main idea. It gives your mind a job to focus on, which helps to quiet all the other noises, worries, memories, and distractions while you are meditating.

Perhaps the most well-known mantra is simply the sound "Om" repeatedly chanted aloud or in our minds. There are many resources available to teach you how to use mantra meditation.

Today, choose a mantra for yourself. You can draw from the Internet, a book, or simply come up with your own. Experiment with using your mantra to meditate.

SEPTEMBER

1
SEPTEMBER

~~~

"We ourselves feel that what we are doing is just a drop in the ocean. But if that drop was not in the ocean, I think the ocean would be less because of that missing drop. I do not agree with the big way of doing things. To us what matters is the individual."

—MOTHER TERESA

2
SEPTEMBER

~~~

Self-love is not permission from our rebellious side to do whatever we want. Following through on our commitments is a way of demonstrating to ourselves that we are important and that we matter. If a coworker or friend was inconsistent in keeping their commitments to you, how hard would it be to trust them? The same goes for building trust with yourself. Show yourself that you can be counted on by following through.

3
SEPTEMBER

~~~

Nourishing our bodies and minds is important. Just as important is nourishing our soul. There are many ways of nourishing your soul, such as singing your favorite song, listening to a guided meditation, reading an uplifting message, doing a random act of kindness, or practicing gratitude. Choose one to try today.

4
SEPTEMBER

~~~

The celebrated pianist and composer Ignacy Jan Paderewski said, "If I miss one day of practice, I notice it. If I miss two days, the critics notice it. If I miss three days, the audience notices it." Whether we are practicing a musical instrument, solving math equations, or wanting a healthier body, it is going to take self-discipline. It seems like such a heavy, exhausting word, and yet, when we practice self-discipline, it sets us free. It opens up possibilities that we didn't have before.

The same can be said for making it a daily practice to express love for yourself and others. This kind of discipline generates all kinds of new possibilities. The freedom you experience, the lessons you learn about yourself and the universe, and the doors opened up to you as a result, will astound you.

5
SEPTEMBER

~

I can overcome anything.

6
SEPTEMBER

~

Close your eyes. In your mind's eye, see the faces of a few people to whom you would turn for comfort and support. Who comes to mind? Now ask yourself: With whom would you celebrate? Which person would you ask for a hug? Who makes you laugh? Who do you enjoy simply being with?

Now consider which of these qualities people might see in you. Perhaps it's your quirky sense of humor. Or people know they can count on you not to scold or judge them when they're going through a rough patch. Some are drawn to quiet thoughtfulness, others to boisterous enthusiasm. Realize that no one can be all things to every person, but you can be the one people turn to for your own delightful, amusing, or comforting qualities.

7
SEPTEMBER

Ancient Polynesian peoples used to travel from island to island in small double-hulled canoes without the use of GPS or a compass.

How did they do it? They memorized where the stars came up and went down along the horizon. This pattern helped them chart the path they had already traversed so that they could make small corrections going forward, until they ended up at their desired destination.

There are times when we may feel lost and cold in the ocean of life. If we feel lost, we can look behind us and see the lights that show us where we have been. Who has been a light in your life? They remind you that you are not alone.

8
SEPTEMBER

"I can accept failure. Everyone fails at something. But I can't accept not trying."

—MICHAEL JORDAN

9
SEPTEMBER

~~~

Are you a perfectionist? Sometimes our perfectionism can get in the way of loving ourselves. It's OK that we want things to be the best they can be; that is a normal human desire. It is also important to recognize that things are rarely *perfect*. It's a wise saying, "Don't let the perfect be the enemy of the good." When we give our expectations a reality check, we can live by greater wisdom. We can appreciate and be content with things that don't reach the peak of perfection, as we imagined, but are *good enough*.

10
SEPTEMBER

~~~

Look in the mirror. Try to look yourself in the eye. It may be difficult. Perhaps you have avoided looking at yourself for a while. That's OK. Do your best to try looking at yourself right now. Then say the following to yourself out loud, three times:

> *May I be well.*
> *May I experience joy, peace, and love today.*
> *May I be free of suffering.*

11
SEPTEMBER

~~~

There is a technique called mirroring, which is basically matching your body position with another person's in a way that doesn't look totally obvious. Mirroring another person is a powerful tool of connection. It helps us not only tune in to the other person, but to ourselves as well. As we match the other person in subtle ways, we deepen our awareness of what might be going on in that person and in ourselves.

Try mirroring someone today. See what happens.

12
SEPTEMBER

~~~

"Nothing is impossible, the word itself says, 'I'm possible!'"

—AUDREY HEPBURN

13

Anger can come from feeling that something has been taken from us without our consent. But we are sometimes afraid to vocalize our anger. We may have even been raised with the message that expressing anger is not OK.

There are times when we hold in our anger to the point that when it does come out, it is raging and scary, which only solidifies the core belief that we shouldn't express our anger at all. But expressing your anger in a healthy way can actually be freeing. Saying you're angry and explaining why can empower you to take action that is more aligned with your value system and desired outcomes.

Expressing anger in a healthy way may be scary for you. Be kind to yourself while exploring the emotion of anger. In your journal, write about a time when you felt angry but held it in. Write about a time when someone expressed anger and respect at the same time. Write about times when anger was expressed in a scary way. What are some of your beliefs about expressing anger?

14
SEPTEMBER

~~~

"I slept and dreamt that life was joy.
I awoke and saw that life was service.
I acted and behold, service was joy."

—RABINDRANATH TAGORE

15
SEPTEMBER

~~~

When we trust ourselves, it is so much easier to be kind and compassionate.
We don't get sucked into the shame and the fear of wondering when someone
is going to reject us. We don't feel like we need to keep secrets. We are free.
Free to love. Free to act with kindness. Free to challenge negative thought
processes. The more we practice kindness, the more willing we are to be honest
with ourselves. The more we are honest with ourselves, the easier it becomes to
practice self-kindness.

16
SEPTEMBER

~~~

Prepare a healthy meal with lots of fresh whole foods in vibrant colors: green, red, yellow, orange, and purple. Enjoy it yourself or share with a loved one.

17
SEPTEMBER

~~~

It was a national cleanup day and citizens in a small neighborhood joined together to tidy up a dilapidated park. Children hadn't played there in a long time. The play equipment was falling apart, weeds had sprouted all over the place, and graffiti was splattered everywhere. The small cleanup crew looked exhausted before they even began. It was going to be a long, hot day.

Suddenly, a truck arrived and a bunch of young adults from the local university jumped out. With music blaring, the people sang and smiled while they worked. In a matter of a few hours, the entire park had been cleaned up.

There's so much that needs doing in our world. Today, put your self-love into practice by realizing how much you have to offer as a volunteer. You could socialize the lonely cats at an animal shelter, hand out food at your local food pantry, usher at a performance hall; there's so much need that you are sure to find an opportunity that matches what you have to offer. With whom could you share your gifts of service?

18
SEPTEMBER

Part of learning to be resilient is recognizing our strengths. Write down as many of your strengths as you can think of. If you run out of ideas, ask someone who loves you.

19
SEPTEMBER

"It has often been observed, that those who have the most time at their disposal profit by it the least. A single hour a day, steadily given to the study of some interesting subject, brings unexpected accumulations of knowledge."

—WILLIAM ELLERY CHANNING

20
SEPTEMBER

~~~

Reflect on one of your mistakes. Don't shy away. We can learn how to do things better when we review the past. How have you grown because of your mistake? Thank yourself for learning this lesson.

21
SEPTEMBER

~~~

We all battle shame. We wrestle with the messages that tell us we are inadequate, powerless, or worthless. Think of a time when the shame was particularly challenging and write down what happened.

As you take a step back from what you wrote, take a moment to identify what you recorded that is 100 percent factual about the situation. Facts are things that you can see, smell, taste, or touch. They are the things that you could see on a video camera. Facts are not our thoughts, feelings, or interpretations. Circle anything you wrote that was factual.

How many circles do you have? Chances are there are relatively few.

Rewrite your story using only the facts you circled. How does it feel to read this new story?

22
SEPTEMBER

~~~

"Staying vulnerable is a risk we have to take if we want to experience connection."

—BRENÉ BROWN, *THE GIFTS OF IMPERFECTION*

23
SEPTEMBER

~~~

Create a time line of difficult experiences in your life. You can go as far back as birth, or keep the time frame more limited. When you are done, look at each event and identify the "angels," or people in your life who provided love, support, protection, or encouragement on your journey. Write each name down in a separate list. As you identify these people, you may realize you have been surrounded by more support than you initially thought. Reflect on this revelation.

24
SEPTEMBER

~~~

I never give up.
I keep moving forward.

25
SEPTEMBER

~~~

There are moments when life seems to slow down completely, the world becomes hushed, and all seems well in the universe. Perhaps it was the time you saw a herd of deer in the forest, their ears turning like antennae before they bounded away. Or when you watched a hummingbird feeding on flowers, buzzing from blossom to blossom to take a sip from each. Perhaps it was when you saw a lightning bug for the first time, or watched the sunset over the ocean. These moments aren't planned, really. They just seem to happen as if by magic. Take some time to reflect on the beauty of the experience. Journal how it makes you feel now.

26

~~~

Our bodies are always trying to tell us things, but we may not always listen as well as we should. Listening takes practice, and this exercise will help you develop your listening skill. Think of a time recently when you experienced intense emotion. Recall the memory and try to recreate the emotion in your body, right now. The more you can feel it, the more knowledge you are likely to gain. Can you name the emotion? If it is unpleasant, is there an attachment wound associated with it? As you allow yourself to feel the emotion, ask your body: *What do you need from me right now?* Then listen. It may take several minutes before you get an answer. Your body is trying to send you a message. What does it need? Perhaps it needs a hug. Maybe it needs a massage. Perhaps it needs water. It could need words of acceptance or a gesture of assurance that all is well. Once you figure out what your body needs, take a step to help it get its need met in a healthy way.

27

~~~

In forgiving, I heal, too.

~~~

Imagine this: You go into a movie theater and sit in the front row. Then you rise out of your body, leaving your body behind in your seat, and float up to the projection booth. You start the movie, and then look out through the glass and down on the version of you sitting in the theater. The movie is a moment-by-moment documentary of your typical morning. The film not only shows what you are doing, but it has an audio recording of your thoughts. The you in the front row is hearing all the gloomy, self-critical thoughts you say about yourself.

As you watch from the booth, notice how the you in the front row feels while watching the film. Can you have compassion for both the you in the film and the you watching it from below? What would you like to say to the you in the front row? What would you like to say to the you in the movie?

This may be a challenging exercise. If you lose focus, take some deep, slow breaths and try again. This exercise creates a forced-perspective experience, a more objective view. You are able to stand back, and then stand back again, to see a much bigger picture. It helps you be less judgmental and more compassionate. This self-observation from a distance can help you along in your healing journey.

29
SEPTEMBER

~~~

**"What would it be like if I could accept life—
accept this moment—exactly as it is?"**

—TARA BRACH, *RADICAL ACCEPTANCE*

30
SEPTEMBER

~~~

In seeking deeper connections with others, it is helpful to understand your own values and where they came from. Self-awareness is an essential part of self-love and loving others. Consider when and how your values and beliefs were developed. Some of them likely originated in your childhood and teenage experiences, but they can also change as you grow. Our fundamental beliefs are established by whatever we have learned, experienced, and lived through.

It is also helpful to be curious about what others believe and where their beliefs come from. As you explore this with others, you will be able to see them more clearly as the individuals they are, rather than through the prism of your value system. In revealing yourself honestly to others, you may gain new insight into who you are, strengthening your self-awareness and self-love.

OCTOBER

1
OCTOBER

~~~

I am working on
trusting myself
more today than
I did yesterday.

2
OCTOBER

~~~

**"Don't believe everything you think.
Thoughts are just that—thoughts."**

—ALLAN LOKOS, *POCKET PEACE*

3
OCTOBER

~~~

Paying attention to what you are doing and why you are doing it strengthens resiliency. This is called being intentional. Think about how you eat, for example. Are you more likely to grab something quick as you're running from one meeting to the next? Or do you slow down and really experience the taste, aroma, and texture of your food before you swallow it?

When we slow things down and consider what we are doing, we build our ability to be patient, which is a part of resiliency. Practice intentional eating today. Try eating something you find absolutely delicious. Slow down and mindfully eat it, savoring every bite.

4
OCTOBER

~~~

Our willingness to face a problem and figure it out is a form of self-compassion. It is our way of saying: *Self, I believe in you. You can do this.*

5

OCTOBER

~~~

It is easy to hate the shadows of shame. We want to hurt them, reject them, or avoid them altogether. But this does not actually bring us peace. When we learn that the shadows of shame are actually just trying in a misguided way to help us, we can respond with loving-kindness.

Instead of shouting, "I hate you," we could try something like this: *I know you're trying to make me perfect so that I don't hurt anymore. But it isn't actually working, and it actually causes me more pain. I am going to make some mistakes along the way and that's OK. When I do, I am going to surround myself with people who love me, and it is all going to be just fine. Thank you for worrying about me. I am going to take care of me now.*

When we respond with loving-kindness, we feel safer and more connected. So if you recognize one of the shadows of shame showing up today, practice loving-kindness toward it. See what happens.

6

OCTOBER

~~~

Take a 30-minute walk today. Breathe in the fresh air. Feel the sunshine on your face and arms. If it's raining, use an umbrella.

7

~~~

Perhaps one of the great challenges of our lives is learning to forgive ourselves.

8

~~~

**"You cannot do a kindness
too soon, for you
never know how soon
it will be too late."**

—RALPH WALDO EMERSON

167

9
OCTOBER

~~~

When a submarine is on the surface of the water, the pilot is able to rely on GPS to navigate where to steer the ship. However, once the submarine dives underwater, the submarine uses an entirely different system including sonar. Sonar sends sounds through the water and then measures how long it takes for the sound to bounce back from objects nearby. But in order for sonar to work effectively, the submarine has to slow down and make relatively little noise, otherwise there is too much interference.

We are similar, in a way. We often are so busy that we have difficulty listening to our bodies or hearing what the universe is trying to communicate to us. So many things distract us.

If the captain of the submarine needs to use sonar, he will order the ship staff to engage in ship quiet procedures. We can do the same for ourselves. Take some time today to free yourself from distractions and meditate with the purpose of listening to what the universe is trying to tell you. It may take some practice, so be patient. There is a message for you today.

10
OCTOBER

~~~

When we look at a star in the night sky, we are actually gazing at light that has traveled thousands of light-years to reach our eyes. (For perspective, each light-year is 5.88 trillion miles.) We are looking at the lasting memory of the star. Even if we don't realize that some of the stars we see no longer exist (indeed, they may have been gone for billions of years), the stars inspire us. Navigators have used them to travel around the globe, and poets, painters, and songwriters have used them as inspiration for their artistry. Scientists have built rockets and telescopes to discover their mysteries. And some have simply enjoyed viewing the heavens just for their sheer mind-boggling immensity.

Like the stars, you have a light within you that has made this world a better place. You have touched others' hearts. You have brightened others' days. Your light may have even helped another find their way.

Even after we have left this planet, our light can be a beacon. How do you want to be remembered? Whose lives do you want to touch?

11
OCTOBER

~

Talk less. Listen more. We have two ears and one mouth for a reason.

12
OCTOBER

~

Western philosophy says: *If you work really hard, you will be successful, and then you can be happy with what you have accomplished.* Eastern philosophy says: *You can be happy in this moment, even if you have not fully reached your goals.*

   Both philosophies have merit. Often our goals push us to try harder in order to realize them. Let's use weight loss as an example. Western philosophy encourages us to celebrate after we have lost a specific number of pounds. Our goal pushes us to lose the weight. Eastern philosophy encourages us to love our bodies the way they are now, in this moment. It is the yin and yang of self-compassion. Working hard toward a goal is important, and loving ourselves helps us along the way.

13
OCTOBER

~~~

Selfishness is a white-knuckled grip we use when we are afraid of losing something we deem valuable. As we tighten the grip, we may put ourselves or others in danger of being hurt. We may not even notice because we are so focused on ourselves.

Self-care, on the other hand, is similar to using a handrail as we climb a staircase. We use it to stabilize ourselves as we are making progress and moving forward. The emphasis is not on ourselves, but rather on having a steadying support so we don't fall down. We are then in a better position to reach behind us to grasp the hand of another person who is climbing the stairs behind us.

14
OCTOBER

~~~

"Anybody can become angry—that is easy, but to be angry with the right person and to the right degree and at the right time and for the right purpose, and in the right way— that is not within everybody's power and is not easy."

—ARISTOTLE

15
OCTOBER

~~~

Place your right hand under your left armpit. Feel the warmth of your arm and your body as they gently enclose your hand. Notice what energy exists in your hand. Notice if any emotion arises. Now move your left hand and put it on the outside of your right shoulder or arm. You may even wish to move the hand up and down. Notice the temperature difference between your left hand and your arm. Notice how it feels to give yourself a hug. Notice any emotions that arise.

After a few minutes, move your left hand to your forehead. What does it feel like to have your hand there? Notice the temperature, the texture, and the sensations. Notice the emotion. Notice what happens to your thoughts. Notice what happens in your heart.

After a few minutes, move your left hand to your belly. Breathe. Continue to notice the temperature, textures, sensations, emotions, and thoughts.

Which position felt most comfortable for you? Return to that position and just hold it for a little while longer, giving yourself permission to enjoy the experience.

16

OCTOBER

~~~

Empathy is a skill that can be taught, just like playing a musical instrument, playing a sport, performing surgery, or changing the oil in a car. For some, empathy comes naturally. For others, it may be a little more difficult. However, regardless of whether a person is born with the skill or needs an introduction and training, feeling empathy for a stranger takes practice.

Try this exercise: Get out a piece of paper and draw a line down the middle. Now think of a time when you got into a disagreement with someone. On the left side of the line, write down how things happened from your perspective. Include what was said and by whom. On the right side of the line, write down as many emotions as you can remember feeling. Then take a short break.

Now put yourself in the other person's shoes. On the left-hand side, write down what happened from *their* perspective. Try to put yourself in their shoes and describe the disagreement as best you can from their point of view. Then, on the right side, write down the emotions you think they felt.

How did it go? What did you learn in doing this activity? Did it shift how you see yourself or the other person?

17
OCTOBER
~

I love myself enough to make healthy choices.

18
OCTOBER
~

There are hundreds of high schools across the country doing away with traditional grades. Instead of getting A's or B's or even F's, students are given colors. Blue means the student has mastered the task; red means "not yet." Imagine that instead of getting a grade that tells you that you are a failure, you get a message that says: *You are on the right track; don't give up.*

The next time you don't reach a goal, instead of telling yourself you failed, try a different message: *Self, you are headed in the right direction. Don't give up. You will get there.*

19

OCTOBER

~~~

"One looks back with appreciation
to the brilliant teachers, but with gratitude to
those who touched our human feelings.
The curriculum is so much necessary raw
material, but warmth is the vital element for the
growing plant and for the soul of the child."

—CARL JUNG

20

OCTOBER

~~~

Connection is essential to our safety and quality of life. We are wired for connection. We are wired to care for others. It is in our DNA. And we will be much better at connecting with others if we are also loving and kind to ourselves.

21
OCTOBER

~~~

Trust that your desires,
your values, your dreams,
and your principles are worthy.

22
OCTOBER

~~~

Shame often hijacks our ability to forgive ourselves. The shadows of shame demand that we continue to be punished for our wrongdoings, even if we have been suffering for years. We rehash, ruminate, and regret, even though we can't turn back time and change what happened. When you are bombarded with these feelings, repeat this mantra: *What was done is done. I cannot change the past. I can only do something now, in this moment, to make a different future. And I am willing to move forward.*

23

OCTOBER

~~~

When we put on a mask, it doesn't lead to joy or peace. Rather, we experience mutated emotions. Anger mutates into rage or resentment. Sadness mutates into depression or apathy. Fear mutates into anxiety. We generally wear a mask because we are hurting. Taking the mask off can be incredibly challenging. It is a courageous act of vulnerability.

Try to identify what pain is under your mask. Is it an attachment wound of abandonment, loss, rejection, neglect, betrayal, or abuse? If you take off the mask, you will have the access you need to attend to the wound that is causing you pain. Even a simple act of kindness can provide tender care for your wounds; but first, you need to take off the mask.

24

OCTOBER

~~~

Resiliency is a skill that can be learned. I am becoming more resilient.

25
OCTOBER

~~~

If you were at a swimming pool and noticed someone drowning, you would immediately take action, getting help or acting to save the person yourself.
   But when you feel like you are drowning in the challenges of life, do you reach for a flotation device, or do the shadows of shame hold you down? If you are feeling overwhelmed, what can you do to extend yourself a lifeline? Can you reach out for help? Can you give yourself a pep talk?

26
OCTOBER

~~~

"The essence of bravery is being without self-deception."

—PEMA CHÖDRÖN, *THE PLACES THAT SCARE YOU*

27
OCTOBER

There is a predictable pattern associated with our attachment wounds.
When our wounds get bumped, we experience anger and want to retaliate,
or we pull away and want to shut down what we are feeling.

Notice whether this happens for you, and acknowledge when your wounds
are bumped. Name how you feel. Slow the process down and ask yourself:
What do I need?

28
OCTOBER

"This a wonderful day.
I've never seen this one before."

—MAYA ANGELOU

29
OCTOBER

~~~

In the Legend of Stone Soup, a weary traveler comes to a small town where there has been a lot of suspicion and animosity among the villagers. The weary traveler knocks on each of the doors, asking if anyone has anything they could share with him to eat. No one will open their doors or even speak with the traveler. He finally gives up and decides to make a small fire in the town square. He pulls out a black cooking pot from his knapsack and fills it with water from the fountain in the square. After placing the pot on the fire, he begins looking around the square for rocks to put in the pot. The villagers have been watching out of their windows, and finally a woman comes out to ask what he is doing.

"I am making stone soup," he says.
"Stone soup? I have never heard of that," says the woman. "Is it delicious?"
"Yes, but it would taste much better if it had carrots."
"I have some of those. I'll go get them." And the woman runs into her house.

Soon other villagers gather. They, too, are willing to add their vegetables to the pot.

In the end, the villagers all share a meal together for the first time in a long time. Is there something you could share with someone today? Sharing is a beautiful way to love someone else while simultaneously feeling love in return.

30
OCTOBER

~

Practicing empathy takes energy, and sometimes we lose track of its vital importance. We can be tempted to settle into our own perspectives and view the world with our own judgments. And sure, it is easier to do that. But it's a lonely and isolated way to live. By practicing empathy, we can avoid or dissolve lasting division and conflict. When you hone your empathy skills, you can discover amazing solutions to problems and enjoy life more fully. Doing so takes effort and dedication, but the rewards will benefit you and everyone around you.

31
OCTOBER

~

"Let's not forget that the little emotions are the great captains of our lives and we obey them without realizing it."

—VINCENT VAN GOGH

NOVEMBER

1
NOVEMBER

~~~

When we have self-trust, it is easier to make healthy choices. We don't get caught up in the shadows of shame telling us what we should or shouldn't do. We don't experience anxiety over getting conflicting messages.

   Take time to consider what choices are in your best interest and the best interest of others, and then choose the course of action that will lead to the greatest joy and freedom. Journal how increasing your self-trust helps you make better decisions.

2
NOVEMBER

~~~

As soon as you have the opportunity today, take a warm, steamy shower or enjoy a relaxing bath. Add Epsom salts and fragrant essential oils to help soothe your muscles and melt the stress away.

3
NOVEMBER

~~~

Write a letter of gratitude to someone who changed your life.

4
NOVEMBER

~~~

Life is going to be bumpy, and as long as you expect to travel smoothly without being jarred or bounced around, you will experience suffering. Indeed, when you accept that you will face challenges at times, you can be better prepared, and you can even acknowledge that the road will at times be painful. You can also acknowledge that you don't travel this road alone; there are people to help you, and perhaps you can even look for someone who needs your help along the way.

5
NOVEMBER

~~~

"This is the single most powerful investment we can ever make in life—investment in ourselves, in the only instrument we have with which to deal with life and to contribute."

—STEPHEN R. COVEY

6
NOVEMBER

~~~

Sometimes we can't forgive ourselves because we have not made restitution for harm we have caused. Restitution is a way of trying to restore what was damaged or lost. Is there someone to whom you would like to make restitution? It can be challenging to identify who it was, the harm you caused, and how that may have impacted them. At the same time, it can shed light on what you can do to restore the trust that was lost. It may become easier to forgive yourself after you feel that you have made some restitution.

7
NOVEMBER

In 1954, a massive Buddha statue made of stucco and glass was to be moved to a new temple in Thailand. But as the construction crew lifted it with the crane, ropes snapped and the statue crashed to the ground.

Worried that serious damage had been done, the workers scrambled to assess the situation. What they discovered was a surprise. The stucco had chipped, revealing gold underneath. Carefully, workers removed the stucco and glass to reveal a solid gold Buddha.

Historians suspect that 200 years previously, the kingdom fell under attack from invaders. The monks watching over the temple wanted to protect the statue, and so, they covered it up with clay, stucco, and glass. The invaders attacked the village and left it in ruins, but the statue was left untouched.

Sometimes we do the same thing to ourselves. Do you recognize your worth or do you cover it up?

8
NOVEMBER

Even a little progress is still progress. Celebrate your steps forward, even if they are baby steps.

9

~~~

If you have ever traveled anywhere, chances are you have encountered the dreaded signs: "ROAD WORK AHEAD. BE PREPARED TO STOP." You have a planned route to your destination, along with the estimated time of arrival, only to discover that the road is closed and you are now being stopped in a long line waiting for the flagger to let you all through, or directed onto a detour. It's easy to get irritated at this change of plan, but allowing yourself to become frustrated only makes the delay even more painful.

Life has a way of throwing us delays, both literally and figuratively. The self-compassionate way of addressing these unexpected roadblocks includes cognitive restructuring. In other words, we have to tell a new, positive, optimistic story about the construction. Instead of saying, "Wow, this construction is really slowing things down," say, "That's fantastic! It gives me time to listen to a little bit more of my audiobook."

Think of a recent negative story you or one of your shadows of shame have told you. Now turn it into a positive one. You get extra points for exaggerated creativity, for example, "I am so glad I was diverted in traffic today. I evaded the Martians who were about to tractor beam me up to their spaceship."

10
NOVEMBER

~~~

I take time to nourish my body,
my heart, my mind, and my soul.

11
NOVEMBER

~~~

It is normal to have fears about being kind to yourself. You may worry that you are being too nice, letting yourself off the hook for things that you believe are important. You may be afraid that being too loving will make you weak and unmotivated to change. Surprisingly, research shows that those who are kind to themselves tend to be more motivated, happier, and more resilient.

Can you practice self-compassion in the face of your fears? First, write down any fears you have about being kind to yourself. Second, reflect on the fears and validate to yourself that it can be scary to practice self-compassion. Third, write a response that is compassionate and encouraging. What would you say to a little child who is terrified to do something new?

12
NOVEMBER

~

There is so much light and goodness in the world. Through gratitude, I provide the glasses through which I can see it.

13
NOVEMBER

~

When our shadows of shame march in to tell us lies that create discouragement, anxiety, confusion, or other dark and challenging emotions, we can ask ourselves three questions: *Is it true, or do I just believe that it is true? Does it help me stand in my light, use my gifts, or be more loving? How do I want to respond to this message or situation in a way that is more loving, kind, and courageous?* Working through these three questions can help us shift out of the darkness and into our light.

14
NOVEMBER

"Often people attempt to live their lives backward: they try to have more things or more money in order to do more of what they want so that they will be happier. The way it actually works is the reverse. You must first be who you really are then do what you need to do in order to have what you want."

—MARGARET YOUNG

15
NOVEMBER

One of the easiest ways to become more grounded and connected with the earth is to take off your shoes. It's even better if you can do this outside where you can feel the grass and earth under your feet, but if you aren't in a place where standing outside is available, then just take your shoes off right now. Wiggle your toes. Feel the ground (or floor) against your feet. Imagine that you grow roots that sink into the ground below you. Anchor yourself while imagining breathing energy from the ground up through your feet and into your body. Spend a few minutes breathing and connecting to the earth.

16
NOVEMBER

When we practice compassion toward a person who is suffering, we feel motivated to do something to relieve their pain. We don't want to punish the person or make them feel worse. We want to help. We want them to know they are not alone in this.

Consider this the next time you are feeling pain yourself. How would you react if your friend or loved one was in the same situation? Try to react with kindness rather than irritation or disappointment that you are suffering, and see if you are able to soothe your pain a little more.

17
NOVEMBER

"If we share our shame story with the wrong person, they can easily become one more piece of flying debris in an already dangerous storm."

—BRENÉ BROWN, *THE GIFTS OF IMPERFECTION*

18
NOVEMBER

~~~

There is a difference between blame and ownership. Blaming is a way of attempting to get rid of pain and discomfort. When our shadows of shame start blaming us, we end up doing the shame two-step. First, we are attacked for being imperfect. Then we take a defensive left step to justify and minimize our behaviors before sliding back into being belittled. We step from side to side, overwhelmed by shame and trying to wiggle out of it without anyone finding out.

Ownership is not a dance. It is a courageous stance. Ownership is taking responsibility for one's actions, understanding their impact, and doing one's best to make amends. Ownership creates an environment where trust can be fostered.

The next time you make a mistake, notice whether you go into self-blame or ownership.

19
NOVEMBER

~~~

When is the last time you cheered for one of your successes? How about cheering right now? Seriously. Stop reading this book, think of something you accomplished today, and celebrate it. Out loud. Right now.

20
NOVEMBER

〜

People can be like tortoises. We often pull our heads into our shell (figuratively) when we feel like someone is going to hurt us. We may even send signals for others to step away if we are feeling unsafe. But if we are offered safety and kindness, chances are much higher that we will engage and emerge from our shell.

You can practice this on yourself, replacing the messages of shame that have made you pull back into your shell with positive truths such as: *I matter, I belong,* or *I am worthy of love.*

21
NOVEMBER

〜

"The present moment is filled with joy and happiness. If you are attentive, you will see it."

—THÍCH NHẤT HẠNH, *PEACE IS EVERY STEP*

22

~~~

The irony of resilience is that it cannot be built without something to push against. You won't become more fit by lifting one-pound weights. Even if you do 50 reps with a one-pound weight, the muscles are not going to grow because they need resistance. The muscles need to be stressed. You usually do this by starting with a heavier weight, one that can you can lift eight to 10 times with moderate difficulty. As your muscles begin to grow and get stronger, you'll increase the weight.

The same principle applies to our ability to handle tough challenges. A necessary part of self-love is building resiliency, and we won't build much resilience without working through hard things. As much as we would love to sail through life without any problems, we don't learn anything that way, and we miss out on the practice of being kind and compassionate. We miss out on perspective.

How has going through something really hard made you a more loving and compassionate person?

23
NOVEMBER

～

Our brains and our bodies are designed to help us survive, both individually and as a species. But there is no adaptive survival benefit for us, as a species or in our personal lives, in allowing the shadows of shame to hijack our lives and convince us to be small. We can disagree with those dark messages. We can speak the truth. We can feel joy.

24
NOVEMBER

～

We often focus on the differences between ourselves and others, and we often fail to find similarities, especially when we view someone as not belonging to our group (race, religion, political views, place of employment, and so on). Consider for a moment someone who is different from you or does not belong to your identified group.

Make a list of all the things that you have in common, and then a list of differences between you. Which list is longer?

This exercise may help you see you have more in common than you thought, but it may also show you the ways in which your differences can actually be assets. How can you learn from this person's different perspective, background, or knowledge? What can they learn from you?

25
NOVEMBER

~~~

We often are more harsh, critical, and judgmental of ourselves than anyone else on the planet. And when we are judgmental or critical of others, it is often because that person is revealing parts of our self that trouble us. But you have a light inside of you that is meant to be seen. Be kind to yourself, and you will make the world a better place.

26
NOVEMBER

~~~

"In uniting the beloved life to ours we can watch over its happiness, bring comfort where hardship was, and over memories of privation and suffering open the sweetest fountains of joy."

—GEORGE ELIOT, *DANIEL DERONDA*

27
NOVEMBER

〜

"It takes courage to grow up
and become who you really are."

—E. E. CUMMINGS

28
NOVEMBER

〜

There is a difference between shame and guilt. Shame says: *You are bad, defective, and worthless.* Guilt says: *You made a mistake that may have caused pain to yourself or others.* Shame is toxic and causes us to hide, pull away, or attempt to cover up our behaviors. Guilt, on the other hand, is incredibly healthy when it inspires us to want to make changes, correct our mistakes, or rebuild trust. Think about a time when you made a mistake recently. Are you feeling more shame or more guilt? If you are battling shame, you may want to reach out to someone who can help you remove the shame so that you can move forward with forgiveness and self-compassion.

29
NOVEMBER

~~~

Fred Rogers, of *Mister Rogers' Neighborhood,* taught volumes about being loving, kind, and fully present. He observed, "People are simple and deep, but the world makes us shallow and complicated." You are a being of incredible depth. You impact the world in simple and yet profoundly meaningful ways. Now, the world does its best to run interference. It bombards you with social media posts and advertising, conveying messages that you are not enough unless you buy or engage in certain products or activities. It's easy to become embroiled in petty dramas that drain you.

Step away from the hustle and bustle of the world for a moment. Take a minute to ground yourself and repeat a mantra that Mr. Rogers would endorse: *I am simple and deep.*

30
NOVEMBER

~~~

Sometimes we are willing to settle for things rather than create a fuss. We worry that if we ask for what we want, we will cause problems or be turned down. But remember, the worst thing that someone can say when you ask for something is no. Is there anything in your life you've been settling for? Can you ask for help or an adjustment so that you get closer to what you truly want? Show your self-love by advocating for yourself today.

DECEMBER

1
DECEMBER

My actions match my words.

2
DECEMBER

Do you ever get so excited to accomplish a goal that you get overwhelmed by where to start? Perhaps you've gone to a conference or learned something new that has inspired you to make a change. Your motivation levels skyrocket, and you are ready to start, only to find that a few days later, the motivation leaks out like air from a punctured tire. Why is it sometimes so hard to sustain the momentum?

When looking broadly at a goal, it can be difficult to see a path forward. This leaves you feeling overwhelmed and as though you have failed before you've even begun. Instead, ask yourself: *What is one thing I can do consistently that will help me get to my desired future outcome?* Just one thing. Move forward from there. How long can you commit to this one thing before you add something else? Can you make the commitment with someone else to hold you accountable?

Taking some time to think through and plan will lead to greater success than just running with emotion. Emotion comes and goes. Energy comes and goes. Making and keeping small commitments eventually leads to amazing outcomes.

3
DECEMBER

You've surely heard the biblical saying, "The truth will set you free." This is just as true when we are honest with ourselves. When we stand in the light of truth, we can more clearly see the deception of the shadows. Truth helps us make rational choices grounded in reality. Truth is empowering.

4
DECEMBER

"To keep a lamp burning, we have to keep putting oil in it."

—MOTHER TERESA

5
DECEMBER

~~~

When the cabin pressure of an airplane changes and the oxygen bags drop down, adults are instructed to put their own oxygen mask on before helping their children. This may go against the parent's instinct; they want their child to be safe and cared for. But without securing their mask, they won't be able to help as effectively.

Doing our own work, looking out for our interests, is a key part of self-compassion; it makes us more effective in being fully present to provide support to someone else. What does doing your own work look like for you?

6
DECEMBER

~~~

When we embrace our positive core truth and breathe it in, there's a fundamental shift in how we see suffering. When we find a purpose for why we have gone through what we have gone through, it changes our behavior. When we accept that we are worthy of love and belonging, no matter what, we become unstoppable.

7
DECEMBER

Deep within you is your core self. It is the embodiment of who you truly are. It is a place of wisdom, courage, assertiveness, and power. It is that part we must explore and share with others to enable more intimate connections and growth.

Close your eyes and begin a quiet meditation. Scan your body from the top of your head down to your toes until you can find where your core self dwells. It may take a few minutes to find it. Be patient and breathe. Once you have discovered it, notice its surroundings. Is it locked behind a prison wall? Is it open and free? Is it easy for you to connect with?

Throughout the day, take a few moments to access your core self. Try to connect with it a handful of times. At the end of the day, journal what that was like for you. What did you learn? What was intriguing? What was difficult? What was easy?

8
DECEMBER

I can change my beliefs today.

The shadows of shame are really good at telling us what we should and shouldn't do. Write down some of the shoulds that you often hear. Now, take your writing utensil, scratch out the words "you should" or "you shouldn't," and insert the words: "I really want to" or "I really don't want to." At the end of the sentence, write the word "because" and complete the thought. For example: "I shouldn't drink soda" becomes: "I ~~shouldn't~~ really don't want to drink soda because I know it isn't healthy for me." Or expand on that thought: "I ~~shouldn't~~ really want to drink soda because it tastes so yummy even though I know it isn't a healthy choice for me."

When we rewrite the sentence, it helps us see the underlying motive of the shadows. They are trying to help us, but not in a loving or supportive way. Taking a moment to look deeper and reframe this thought does two important things. First, it helps us see a hidden truth. Second, it gives us a few more seconds to evaluate our situation and make a more loving choice. Try this whenever you feel bombarded by these judgmental messages.

10
DECEMBER

~~~

I attract truth, integrity, and light.

11
DECEMBER

~~~

Consider the order of our solar system and the life on our planet. Every day, as the earth turns, the sun rises and falls in a predictable pattern. The earth's tilt brings us the seasons as it makes its annual journey around the sun. We can plant tiny seeds in the right season and know just which foods we will harvest and flowers we can enjoy. Ocean tides can be predicted and charted for every part of the shoreline. Even the lunar and solar eclipses follow long multiyear cycles, so we know precisely when they'll happen and which areas we can view them from.

What does all this mean? There are, perhaps, many answers to that question, but one is that the world can be a safe place. Even amid the chaos, there is predictability. Can you identify areas of your world that are reliable and can be trusted?

12
DECEMBER

~~~

**"In my relationships with persons I have found that it does not
help, in the long run, to act as though I were something I am not."**

—CARL ROGERS, *ON BECOMING A PERSON:
A THERAPIST'S VIEW OF PSYCHOTHERAPY*

13
DECEMBER

~~~

Throughout this book, we have referred to attachment wounds (which linger after
loss, rejection, abandonment, neglect, betrayal, and abuse). Part of life's journey is
learning how to heal those wounds, especially through self-compassion.

As you strive to treat yourself with self-compassion, gently notice when you
may be repeating any of the behaviors that you are trying to heal from. If others
have neglected you, now you can give yourself and others loving attention. If others
have let you down, follow through on your own commitments. And if you've had
your trust betrayed, you can now be a loyal friend to yourself and others.

14
DECEMBER
~

Picking the scabs on physical wounds delays healing and opens them up to infection. The same can be said about our attachment wounds. Wounds begin to heal, but then the little kid in us becomes curious to see what's under there, so we pick it off. We can pick at emotional scabs by bringing up resentments, becoming passive-aggressive or just plain aggressive, falling out of integrity with accountability partners, and similar behaviors.

A good way to avoid picking physical scabs is by putting a bandage over them. By the same token, you can wrap emotional scabs in messages of love by writing compassionate words of encouragement to yourself. You may schedule time to be present with yourself, doing something you find comforting or soothing. You may simply place your hands over your wounded spot and imagine healing light traveling from your hands to that part of your body. What can you do to protect your wound while creating a more healing atmosphere?

15
DECEMBER
~

Say this to yourself 25 times today: *I love you (<u>insert your name</u>). You are a being of light and power. You can achieve whatever it is you are striving for.*

16
DECEMBER

~~~

Namaste: The Spirit in me bows to the Spirit in you.

17
DECEMBER

~~~

Many of us operate under a false premise, believing that humans are selfish and make rational decisions primarily in their own self-interest. This premise fuels actual selfishness; it promotes a scarcity mentality that there will not be enough for everyone.

In fact, we are more prosperous when we have healthy connections, when we feel a sense of belonging, and when we can make a difference in others' lives. Happiness is not created by money; rather, it is created by our loving connections with others.

18

~~~

"I know, Your Honor, that every atom of life in all this universe is bound up together. I know that a pebble cannot be thrown into the ocean without disturbing every drop of water in the sea. I know that every life is inextricably mixed and woven with every other life. I know that every influence, conscious and unconscious, acts and reacts on every living organism, and that no one can fix the blame. I know that all life is a series of infinite chances, which sometimes result one way and sometimes another. I have not the infinite wisdom that can fathom it, neither has any other human brain."

—CLARENCE DARROW, *ATTORNEY FOR THE DAMNED: CLARENCE DARROW IN THE COURTROOM.*

19
DECEMBER

~~~

Neuroscience research confirms what theorists have long believed: We are wired for connection. We impact each other far deeper than we consciously realize. Research has shown that we can shut down our empathic emotional responses based on our judgments, particularly when we don't see that a person belongs in our tribe. We see this very clearly in politics. We are unwilling to listen to what another person has to say simply because they are not part of our political tribe. We make assumptions, judgments, and barriers because we do not perceive that they are part of humanity.

This division creates suffering at neurological levels, which only invites us to become numb. If we really want to practice self-love, we can become curious about how we see the world. Do we engage in behaviors that reject, dismiss, belittle, or dehumanize others simply because they are different from ourselves? Can we be open to the fact that our behavior actually perpetuates our own personal suffering? Perhaps we can be kinder to ourselves and to those we perceive as the enemy.

20
DECEMBER

~~~

The story is told about three bricklayers working out in the hot sun. A man, curious to know what they were building, asked the first man about the project.

"I have no idea," the first man said. "I just show up and do what I am told. It's a job, you know." Still curious, the man asked the second bricklayer what they were building. "We're just building a wall," the bricklayer replied.

The third bricklayer stood up and looked the man in the eye. "Sir, we are not building a wall, we are building a cathedral. And it is my honor to do it."

Three bricklayers with three different attitudes. Which one was the most inspiring? We, too, are bricklayers. We are constructing our lives brick by brick. Step back and see the glorious life you have been building. Notice how your behavior and your outlook may change when you shift your perspective to one of majestic purpose. A broader and longer view of your life and your place in the world is an important support in strengthening your self-love.

21
DECEMBER

~~~

"The best way to find out if you can trust somebody is to trust them."

—ERNEST HEMINGWAY

22
DECEMBER

~~~

Every year, for more than 200 years, the United States Military Academy at West Point has a curious tradition. During graduation, the lowest-ranking cadet to meet the criteria to graduate becomes the "Goat." It may seem like an insult, but in fact it is a celebration. All the other graduates pool their money and award the Goat with the money when he or she receives his or her diploma.

Why would there be such a celebration for coming in last place? Because it is the celebration of tenacity and grit. The Goat never gave up and he or she crossed the line. Some of West Point's previous "goats" have become great leaders in their fields.

An award for being the best is not any more reliable an indicator of future success than coming in last. What really matters is that we keep moving forward.

23
DECEMBER

~~~

You may be familiar with essential oils. They are compounds extracted from plants with healing and empowering properties. Many oils assist us in connecting with the core truth that we are enough and worthy of love and belonging. Some of these include bergamot, frankincense, rose, myrrh, sandalwood, rosewood, chamomile, and rosemary. These can be used individually or in combination. You can use them in a diffuser, or dilute them with a carrier oil to apply to your skin, rubbing clockwise around your chest and belly while saying positive affirmations (essential oils should never be applied undiluted).

24
DECEMBER

~~~

"With all its sham, drudgery, and broken dreams, it is still a beautiful world. Be cheerful. Strive to be happy."

—MAX EHRMANN, *DESIDERATA*

25
DECEMBER

~~~

When we rewrite the negative stories of our past wounds, we shift our perspective. We no longer have to hold onto the mutated emotions of resentment, depression, bitterness, and despair. Write about one of your attachment wounds from the perspective of courage, compassion, faith, and hope. Perhaps share it with a close friend or loved one if you feel comfortable doing so.

26
DECEMBER

~~~

Write down three things that made you laugh today. Journal about what made it so funny or enjoyable. Did you share the laugh with others?

27
DECEMBER

~~~

There is an art to pruning: trimming branches, buds, or roots of a tree or plant so that it can grow more abundantly, or removing damaged or diseased parts of the plant.

For the novice gardener, this can be challenging. We may resist cutting into living wood. The experienced gardener knows that the tree must be pruned. Perhaps an overgrown tree is a safety hazard, or the gardener wants to stimulate more fruits and flowers.

Like the novice gardener, we may be reluctant to let go of parts of ourselves that are no longer serving us: a negative thought, a habit that prevents us from being as healthy and vibrant as we want. But it is courageous to prune the parts of ourselves that no longer serve us. And when we remove the heavy branches and dead wood, we allow more light and air to pass through our branches. We can stand taller, unburdened by heavy old limbs. Pruning these parts affirms that we no longer need them, and our courage and resolve strengthens our self-love, and our capacity to love others.

Is there something in your life no longer serving you? What support do you need so that you can prune it and become freer?

28
DECEMBER

~~~

"I celebrate myself, and sing myself, And what I assume you shall assume, For every atom belonging to me as good belongs to you."

—WALT WHITMAN, *SONG OF MYSELF*

29
DECEMBER

~~~

You have the capacity to look in the mirror and see your beauty. Look for your light. Gaze upon your gifts. Be curious about why your eyes are a certain color or why an image awakens your emotions. We can see ourselves with loving-kindness. What makes you beautiful?

30
DECEMBER

～～～

You have been learning the power of self-compassion and self-love. You've gotten to know yourself better and found ways to begin freeing yourself from old wounds, old beliefs, and old behavior patterns. This didn't happen overnight, of course (and your efforts to grow your self-love will continue for a lifetime), but look how far you've come.

31
DECEMBER

～～～

"[We] don't look backwards for very long. We keep moving forward, opening up new doors and doing new things, because we're curious . . . and curiosity keeps leading us down new paths."

—WALT DISNEY

Acknowledgments

Thank you to the researchers and educators (including Tara Brach, Brené Brown, Kelly McGonigal, and Kristen Neff) who have heightened the awareness of the scientific basis for practicing self-love. Your work has guided my work.

About the Author

Troy L. Love is on a quest to help individuals, couples, and organizations find greater peace, joy, happiness, and success. He is a two-time Amazon best-selling author of *Finding Peace: A Workbook on Healing from Loss, Rejection, Neglect, Abandonment, Betrayal, and Abuse* and *The Art of Peace.*

Troy serves as the President and Clinical Director of Yuma Counseling Services. He is also the President of Finding Peace Consulting, LLC. He has over 20 years of experience in the mental health field. Troy received his Master's Degree In Social Work from the University of Pittsburgh in 2000, and much of his training has focused on addiction recovery. He also received certification in Human Resource Studies from Cornell University. He recently completed certification as a sexual addiction treatment professional from Mid-Nazarene University.

He uses his unique set of skills to help individuals who are seeking personal healing and organizations that are seeking to improve outcomes. Troy's workshops, lectures, and group discussions have helped hundreds of people explore sensitive issues, increase understanding, and take action toward change. His down-to-earth, humorous teaching style helps participants feel safe enough to examine their core issues required for change.

Troy resides in Yuma, Arizona with his wife, two children, and two dogs.

To learn more about Troy or to get a free copy of *The Art of Peace,* visit www.TroyLLove.com.

CPSIA information can be obtained
at www.ICGtesting.com
Printed in the USA
LVHW070750150222
710254LV00007B/5

9 781641 527644